WHIRLED
VIEWS

WHIRLED VIEWS

*Tracking Today's
Culture Storms*

MARVIN OLASKY
JOEL BELZ

CROSSWAY BOOKS • WHEATON, ILLINOIS
A DIVISION OF GOOD NEWS PUBLISHERS

Library of Congress Cataloging-in-Publication Data

Olasky, Marvin N.
  Whirled views : tracking today's culture storms / Marvin Olasky
and Joel Belz.
     p.   cm.
  A collection of editorials which previously appeared in World
magazine between 1987-1996.
  ISBN 0-89107-938-6
  1. Christianity and culture. 2. Church and social problems.
I. Belz, Joel, 1941-   II. Title.
BR115.C8043   1997
261'.0973—dc21   96-51913

06	05	04	03	02	01	00	99	98	97
15	14	13	12	11	10	9	8	7	6	5	4	3	2	1

To the readers and supporters of *World*
who made it possible for the magazine to survive
during the early years when most magazines die

CONTENTS

Recently a major presidential candidate was asked if he read the Bible. "I don't have time," he answered dismissively. Too bad for him. Too bad for the country, too. It's not just that his policies were muddled, confused. His explanation of those policies was just as garbled.

He apparently did not know that some of our greatest presidents took inspiration from the Bible. George Washington quoted from 1 Kings 4:25 when he told the Hebrew congregation at Newport in 1790 that he sought a country in which "each can sit under his own vine and fig tree and there will be none to make him afraid." Abraham Lincoln's famous "House Divided" speech in 1858 made him a national figure. A biblically literate people recognized the reference to Mark 3:25.

The Bible has shaped our life as a people throughout our history. As Christian citizens, we do not seek to impose biblical solutions to all political questions so much as we are inspired by the Bible's truth and its wisdom to seek after righteousness. Our country hungers for righteousness. In our day, that word is hardly used at all. It would be virtually impossible to find any reference in the secular media to righteousness that is not a reference to self-righteousness.

Joel Belz and Marvin Olasky are anything but self-righteous. Steeped as they are in the truths of Holy Scripture, they seek to persuade fellow believers to seek the good of the city. This series of their columns and speeches is as winsome as it is winning. I have not always agreed with them on every point of policy. For instance, I believe it is indispensable for the success of the pro-life cause that the Republican party maintain its commitment to a human life amendment. But I do agree most heartily with them that we expect more from our political leaders than a whispered assurance of future support for a hypothetical measure. We want a commitment of the heart that our leaders will, in fact, lead.

These essays originally appeared in *World* magazine. I am often asked for recommendations by young college students confronted with political correctness on campus. I unhesitatingly recommend *World* to them. It is intelligent, well-written, and honest journalism. Joel and Marvin are to be congratulated for shepherding this remarkable Christian publication. It is making a real difference in our country.

What strikes me most about these essays is their refreshing candor. The authors do not claim to have answers for every one of life's heartbreaks or the world's injustices. But they do have the right questions: What would Christ have me do in this situation? This work shows two contemporary leaders struggling with their consciences and taking a bold stand for faith, family, and freedom. I believe that their example can inspire others. It has certainly encouraged me.

Opening Thoughts

Jesus Monster Stories

BY MARVIN OLASKY

JULY 16, 1994

My youngest son, Benjamin, who is three, worried me last month when he said at bedtime, "Don't tell me a Jesus story tonight. I want a monster story."

It seems that I had fallen into an alternating pattern of bedtime stories. Some nights we read and talked about Jesus who taught and then fed thousands, who healed ten men with leprosy, who told about the good Samaritan, who rose from the dead. Other evenings ended with stories about knights and fire-breathing dragons, or sometimes (in our mixing of genres) cowboys lassoing monsters.

To my mind, Jesus' miracles were the more exciting of the stories, without being scary before bedtime. But Benjamin preferred tales of creepy things—monsters in tales, insects in real life—vanquished by heroes. (We have some big bugs in Texas; my oldest son used to pick up invading tree roaches by "the antlers.")

Faced with Benjamin's request, I stopped alternating Jesus stories and monster tales and began telling him a series of "Jesus monster stories." For example, in chapter 5 of Mark (and chapter 8 of both Luke and Matthew) there's a man filled with evil spirit monsters. The man is so strong that he tears off his chains. He's so sad that he cries out and cuts himself with stones. But Jesus is stronger, and Jesus is very kind to the man: Jesus tells the monsters to get out, and they do. They run into pigs, and the pigs rush into a lake and are drowned, and the monsters do not bother that man anymore. The end.

Similarly, in chapter 9 of Mark (and also in Matthew 17 and Luke 9) a daddy has a problem: an evil monster has taken over his son. The monster inside the son makes him foam at the mouth, gnash his teeth, and become rigid. The monster even throws the boy into fire, which can burn you, or water, where you can drown unless you learn how to swim. But the dad asks Jesus for help, and Jesus is strong and kind. Jesus says to the monster, "I command you, come out of him and never enter him again." And the monster yells and comes out, and the boy and his dad are happy. The end.

Benjamin has now heard other Jesus monster stories from the Gospels. He's also heard about Philip and Paul driving out monsters in Acts 8 and 16, and about the battle against monsters in Revelation. His renewed excitement in hearing Bible stories leads me to ponder recent trends in children's books.

At the American Booksellers Association convention last month, the long-term tendency to make children's stories reflect the evening news continued. There were books on divorce, wife and child abuse, and so on. In many of the books it seems as if no one's right and no one's wrong. Things just happen. The father walks out. The kidnapper cometh. The rapist returns. There's no protection against evil, no reason for it, and not even much rhyme in these sad books for sophisticated kids.

In the output of some publishers at the Christian Booksellers Association convention last week, however, the other extreme is evident. One "beginning reader" book about the Exodus has colorful drawings of Egyptians chasing Israelites across the Red Sea. There's tension in the text also: "'Hurry up,' said the people. 'Hurry up!'" But when we turn the page, the water has rolled back, with no mention of massive Egyptian drowning. A pop-eyed Pharaoh stands on the opposite bank, but the Egyptian soldiers have simply disappeared for a time, perhaps soon to reappear.

Other books in an early reader series tell the story of hiding the baby Moses without mentioning Pharaoh's murderous intentions, and the story of Noah without mentioning why God sent a flood or what happened to those outside the ark. In a book titled *Bing!* David bings Goliath on the head with a pebble; the giant is woozy. Since there is no mention of David cutting off Goliath's head, a child might wonder whether there will be a rematch.

These monster stories lack true monsters and do not make clear their demise. The stories show part of God's love, but they omit his holiness.

Some secular psychologists have pointed out the usefulness of semi-gruesome fairy tales: children know there is danger in the world, and they need to have a feeling of control over it. But Christian understanding, based on real biblical history, goes deeper: there is danger in the world, and sometimes we cannot overcome it in our own power, but Jesus can in his.

In other words, the best stories for children are not those that pretend all is well, but those that show how all can be well with Christ. If we minimize Satan's power, we minimize the need for salvation. Children learn early on that evil spirits crouch at their door. To be truly thankful, they need to understand what the apostle John writes: "You, dear children, are from God and have overcome them, because the one who is in you is greater than the one who is in the world" (1 John 4:4).

There will be many monsters in Benjamin's life, so I am glad that during the past week he has been praying before dinner, "Thank you, God, for this food, and for keeping me safe from monsters and snakes. Amen."

Biscuits and Knives

BY JOEL BELZ
APRIL 21, 1986

Our eight-year-old looked at me with astonishment. Sitting just to my left at the dinner table, she had been attacking a wonderfully tender biscuit with her dinner knife. "Don't cut it with your knife," I told Elizabeth. "Use your fingers, and break it apart."

Use my fingers?

Elizabeth, more than anyone at our table, had been reminded dozens of times in recent months not to use her fingers, but her silverware instead. How arbitrary can all these rules be? I could feel the same bewildered question ringing the table.

Emily Post and Amy Vanderbilt got a good going over the next few minutes as we explored whether the "don't-cut-your-biscuit-with-your-knife" rule was indeed arbitrary or if it was rooted in some more basic principle.

"I think," I proposed, not particularly fearing to wade in where I knew nothing at all, "that it probably has to do with showing what you think of the cook. Biscuits are supposed to be tender, not tough. If you use your knife on your biscuit, you're telling the cook that her biscuits are tough—that she was a failure in making them the way they were supposed to be."

Soon, however, another dimension of the whole subject hit the dinner table. Whether or not the etiquette books ever laid arbitrary rules on us, what about God's intentions? Are his commandments, instructions, and rules just something he dreamed up to clutter our lives with things impossible or inconvenient to remember? Or are they rooted in deeper significance?

God's written Word and even his creation sometimes seem arbitrary. To some, the arbitrariness is there when they hear God say, "Sex is right only with the person you're married to." To others, that rule makes sense, but they struggle when God says, "The tithe is mine." You may be faithful to your spouse and a regular tither but still wonder why God prohibited the Israelites in Deuteronomy 22:11 from wearing clothes made of both linen and wool. Admit it: Doesn't that rule prompt you to look up from the dinner table in amazement?

It should. When we quit being astonished at the complexity of what God has ordered in his creation, we've missed his purpose in putting us here. His rules for us as individuals, for society at large, and for his creation are never willy-nilly. Every one of them means something. The sooner we find out what they mean, the more we can revel in his greatness and goodness.

The no-knife-to-the-biscuit rule turns the eater's thoughts to the biscuit's creator. A few days later I asked Elizabeth if that still made sense. She said it did, but that night I had to remind her to use her fork with her casserole.

Jesus the Reverse Immigrant

BY MARVIN OLASKY
DECEMBER 24, 1994

The debate over immigration during this Christmas season reminds me of how I am three times an immigrant, and how one person who has befriended me is the most unusual immigrant of all time.

First, I am by blood a civic immigrant. My grandparents courageously came to America early in this century from thousands of miles away, leaving behind family and familiar environs. They came from an empire of unchecked tyranny and pledged allegiance to a constitution devoted to limiting government; they learned the customs of their new country. One of my earliest memories is of my grandfather taking me to baseball games.

Second, I am by ideology a political immigrant. Two decades ago I moved from the left to the right. I knew then and I've seen since that some conservatives who preach about virtue may be hypocritical, but at least they do not use governmental force to push others to sin. That's the key. Although non-Christian conservatives do not understand the origins and true nature of sin, they see its consequences and are unlikely to buy government-surplus stain removers that in practice grind the evil deeper into the social fabric.

Third and most important, I am by grace an immigrant to Christianity; not until 1976 did I first celebrate Christ's birth. Now, I know, theologically, that everyone is an immigrant to Christ—each believer had to be born again. But I still say, to parallel Paul's words in Romans 3, "What advantage is there in growing up in a Christian home? Much in every way. First of all, they have been entrusted with the very words of God." To grow up with the Gospel, to absorb from an early age the great hymns and confessional statements of the church, and even (on a far lower level) to have warm memories of Christmas is indeed a great privilege.

I'm struck, however, by the number of people who grew up in these three groups and now are embarrassed by them.

Some native-born Americans are chagrined at this country's prosperity. The counterculture's urge to blame America first and praise China, Cuba, or Albania has diminished, but this month singer Pete Seeger received from President Clinton a "medal for lifetime achievement in the performing arts." Seeger at mid-century was at least an FOCP (friend of the Communist Party) and apparently has not changed, except that the decrease in Marxist countries to praise has left him chasing fantasies in the fourth dimension. "When anybody says I'm a Communist," the *New York Times* reported him as commenting, "I say, 'Yup, just like the American Indian.' There was no thievery . . . among the Indians." Right.

Some conservatives so crave the praise of the liberal press that they "grow in office." Look at Supreme Court Justice Anthony Kennedy—now known as "Flipper"—who changed his position on abortion in order to please the editors of the *Times* and the *Washington Post*. Jesse Helms speaks undiplomatically at times, but you can bet that he won't stop dancing with the people and principles that brung him.

Some Christians despise the rich history of the Christian church. These days lots of people demand Scripture songs rather than the great hymns, and times of sharing rather than Bible studies. Some pastors become ministers of entertainment and worry about using un-cool words like *sin*. The excuse that's sometimes offered is: We don't want to scare away potential immigrants. What "church lite" promoters do not understand is that true immigrants want the real thing.

To an immigrant like myself, the abandonment of birthright seems incredible. But I know that those who have been home all their lives may not realize they live in the "better place" immigrants fight and die to come to. We all know that immigrants do not deliberately move to a worse place. Bangladesh does not have a problem with illegal immigrants. Border guards at the Berlin Wall did not have their guns turned on West Germans trying to move from powerful affluence to chained poverty.

That's what makes the Christmas history so compelling. It is a story of reverse immigration—from omnipotence to helplessness. One of the central Reformed documents, the Westminster Shorter Catechism, summarizes the matter in its answer to question 27, "How was Christ humiliated?" The response: He was humiliated "by being born as a man and born into a poor family; by being made subject to the law and suffering the miseries of this life, the anger of God, and the curse of death on the cross; and by being buried and remaining under the power of death for a time."

Here's to a reverse immigrant who deserves all the power and glory and honor. Merry Christmas!

Pick Your Own Jury

BY JOEL BELZ
OCTOBER 14, 1995

Almost fifty years ago a big brick courthouse in Waterloo, Iowa, handed me my first disappointment with civil justice. I sat with my father and my grandfather while a judge ruled against them in a tax case having to do with the grain business they owned together. I was only five years old, but I learned that a building's impressive looks and a judge's authoritative appearance weren't enough to ensure that things would go the way they were supposed to. My father and grandfather were honest businessmen, and they were grieved that their government treated them unfairly.

Thirty years later, a van operated by the Christian high school where I was headmaster was involved in a minor fender-bender—but not so minor that the driver of the other car didn't sue. Four times I took five students from their classes for the whole morning to serve as witnesses in the court case that followed. Four times the party suing the school and its insurance company failed even to show up in court. And four times, inexplicably, the judge continued the case. The students learned a great deal more about American courts than I wanted them to.

A decade ago a hospitalized friend was raped in the middle of the night by a male nurse in the intensive care unit of a local hospital. The criminal and civil cases that followed over the next few years made cynics of most of us who stood by our friend. Looking for justice, she instead got mere scraps thrown out the back door of a traveling circus.

Last week, in the wake of the O.J. Simpson trial, there were some folks who were happy their famous friend had been freed. But even among those who were rejoicing, no one was saying, "Look how well the system works!"

For the fact is that the system no longer works. The whole idea of a process thoughtfully assembled through the centuries was to gather components in careful balance that would punish wrongdoers while also protecting the rights of the innocent. All apart from the specific results of the Simpson trial, many Americans have lost their confidence that such justice prevails.

Why shouldn't they? When righteous government shows itself so elusive, when educational systems have rotted to the core, when the term *business ethics* strikes many as an oxymoron, when the great old institutions fail us, why should we be surprised when jurisprudence also shows signs of collapse?

Here we need to make a key distinction. Whether we're talking about government, education, business, or the administration of justice, the big problem is never in the details of how the task gets done. The problem with American justice is not primarily with the system or the process. The problem isn't with the rules of evidence and whether the *Miranda* decision puts too great a burden on police. The problem is not with jury selection processes.

The problem is that the people who get put on juries, the people who get chosen as judges, and the people who become policemen and then get called on as witnesses—all these people have been shaped by the governments, the educational institutions, the business ethics, and the systems of justice of our day. The result is that you don't really want, any longer, to put your welfare into the hands of such people. People can't be trusted any longer to produce what we call justice because the basic tools of justice were never put into their hands in the first place.

You can't tell people for two or three generations, as even some theologians have, that truth is relative and that nothing is absolute—and then expect them to produce justice. That's true, just as it is that you can't tell people that truth is relative and expect them to produce good government, worthwhile education, or honest business. So it's not just a little tinkering here and there that is necessary to get our confidence in the court systems back again.

The bottom line is this: Imagine you're on trial for your own life. But before the trial begins, you have a chance to get on a bus or an airplane or enter your doctor's waiting room, to walk through and pick any twelve people at random to serve as the jury that will determine your guilt or innocence. Does it matter to you what kind of teaching those people have had all through their lives on the issue of truth as absolute or merely relative? Does it matter where they went to Sunday school, what kind of Gospel they heard? Does it matter what theory of origins those people hold to, whether it was a wise Creator God or a one-in-a-million chance of fate? Does it matter whether they believe in something called sin?

For in the end, that's what justice is all about. If you would be scared—as I would—to go out and pick your own jury, it's not just the system that's in sad shape. No system of any kind works when the people themselves have lost their way.

Juiced Jurors and Voters

BY MARVIN OLASKY
NOVEMBER 5, 1994

Since I wear glasses, I'm not asked to umpire baseball games very often. The last time was four years ago, when the regular umps failed to show at my oldest son's game—Pete then was thirteen—and even the visually challenged and parentally biased were dragooned into service. The first innings were easy, but then came the dreaded close play: Pete was sliding into home, and the catcher was tagging him. OK, it wasn't Abraham being told to kill Isaac, but it was hard to keep sentiment from clouding my already underachieving eyesight.

Ever since then I've particularly appreciated people committed to making straight calls, even if it means standing against their own relatives and friends. In the 1700s, for example, Jonathan Edwards was not afraid to criticize his own congregant members, even though his sermons led to church shrinkage rather than growth and an eventual bum's rush for himself.

Juror selection in the O.J. Simpson trial illustrates the opposite tendency. I've taught courses in media law and made the usual jokes about skid marks before dead armadillos in the road but none before dead lawyers. And yet, I know that adversarial advocates help jurors avoid premature signals of "out" or "safe." Attorneys with attitude, like magazines with bite, are useful. In the O.J. Simpson case, however, lawyers are working hard to get onto the jury not fair umpires, but people of the race and background likely to be biased in their favor. If there is even a bit of dust swirling around, they suggest, jurors should give the safe sign to whoever seems like a member of their family.

In current election campaigns the politics of favoring your own, regardless of the evidence, are also being played out. For example, the once and probable future mayor of Washington, D.C., Democrat Marion Barry, wants political juror/voters at the ballot box to ignore cocaine videotapes and send an in-your-face message to whites. On the opposite coast Republican Pete Wilson may save his lease on the California governor's mansion by scapegoating immigrants—those other folks—for economic problems made worse by his own tax increases and social liberalism.

The tendency now is to support not those who will be fair umpires, but those who can be bought. Two years ago, when the Bush administration was still in power, much corporate money flowed to Republicans; recently the *New York Times* reported overwhelming support for the Democratic Party, since Clintonians now control the regulatory apparatus. "We take a very pragmatic view," the chairman of the Beneficial Corporation says. "I may have my own personal ideological views, but I don't let them interfere in our decisions where the company contributes." (Beneficial, the biggest corporate contributor of "soft money" through June 30 of this year, gave $397,250 to Democrats and $17,500 to Republicans during that period.)

In the 1700s, citizens were urged to contribute to only those "of establish'd Character for Honesty and Integrity"; now, a reputation for fair umpiring can sink a political career. Given the size of the pot that governments now control, the corporate tendency is sad but rational, and individuals follow similar policies. Members of teachers' unions are to vote for the candidates who will get them more money, Social Security recipients for those who will raise their benefits; on it goes down the line.

The tendency, however, can still be opposed. Biblically, facts of the case and values that are good for the country, not benefits to ourselves or our ethnic groups, should determine our calls on close plays. Christian umpires/jurors might have an impact in the Simpson trial and will be the decisive force in tight elections in California, Michigan, Massachusetts, Tennessee, New York, Texas, Florida, and elsewhere.

On November 8 the typical voter may do what he has been taught and ask, "What's in it for me?" Christians may forfeit a piece of crust from the pie by not becoming a special interest group, but Exodus 23:2 is valuable now as always: "Do not follow the crowd in doing wrong." God tells us not to be biased against either rich or poor; and, rather than scorning those unlike ourselves, we are to avoid oppressing the aliens among us. Biased jurors who vote by skin color and not the facts of the case murder justice.

When I called my son Pete out, he took it well. In life I've messed up on a lot of close calls, but my goal is still to join the great cloud of umpires.

Who Changed?

BY   JOEL   BELZ
JUNE   17,   1995

Three times in the last two weeks I've read short and sad accounts of evangelical Christians whose politics and social concerns are decidedly liberal—and who in their own words feel increasingly cut off from their more conservative brothers and sisters.

"Many politically conservative evangelical Christians," writes Tony Campolo in the March-April issue of *Sojourners*, "have been not too subtly transforming God into a transcendental member of the right wing of the Republican Party. It is not just a matter of their making a biblical case for their political agenda; they seem to be going further than that. They are giving the impression that anyone who disagrees with their agenda is outside the will of God."

Mr. Campolo continues: "This recent development has generated great consternation among many of us who, over the last few decades, have used the word *evangelical* to establish our own religious identity. We now have to ask, Can we continue to use that title?"

It is a sad and even tragic thing, according to the Bible, when the body of Christ is split up into factions.

So if Mr. Campolo is right that we conservatives have excluded him and his more liberal friends from the evangelical world, that is a serious matter. Yet that is exactly his charge: "Those of us who do not agree with the attitudes and political ideology of these renamed fundamentalists are treated by them as something less than legitimate Christians. We, who once considered ourselves evangelicals, are being driven out of the camp and rendered ideologically homeless."

While Mr. Campolo is plaintive in style, writer Tom Sine in the same issue of *Sojourners* is angry and bitter. "In 1978," he says, "Billy Graham, *Christianity Today*, and Wheaton College were at the front of the parade as the discussion of Christian social responsibility was still expanding. Suddenly, seemingly out of nowhere, Jerry Falwell, the Moral Majority, Timothy LaHaye, the Religious Roundtable and others hijacked the evangelical parade and gave it a decisive wrench to the Right. It has never recovered."

Hold on! Who changed? Who deserted whom?

The fact is that the Falwells, the LaHayes, and the Robertsons of the 1990s are barely different people from their counterparts of the 1940s and 1950s—except that they have indeed been "liberalized" a bit, perhaps even by the Campolos, the Sines, and the Ron Siders of that era. Blacks and other minorities now participate regularly in their institutions and their movements; significant social welfare aims have been developed as parts of their ministries; and they all have become at least a bit more global and less nationalistic in their emphases. These are all healthy developments—for which "liberals" within evangelicalism deserve credit. I publicly thank them for reminding us that racial discrimination, coldness toward the poor, and arrogant nationalism are all sins addressed by the Bible; they were also all sins within evangelicalism that needed (and still need) attention.

But at the same time, two other entities were changing radically.

Society itself seemed to be losing its moorings. A *Time* magazine cover proclaimed the death of God. A new morality relativized right and wrong. Three assassinations of key figures and several other near misses rocked people's sense of confidence in a stable political order. The Supreme Court changed its whole character to become not an interpreter of the law but an activist law-making body. In short, the whole idea of trustworthy authority was taking it on the chin.

For anyone to argue that all these developments, and many like them, should not have alarmed Christian people, used to a nominal assent by society to biblical standards, is to ignore a huge chunk of American history.

Meanwhile, a second movement was taking a parallel toll. While eager secularists were chopping away at the traditional authority structures of society at large, some evangelical leaders were doing precisely the same thing for their followers. "The Bible doesn't really mean what you always thought it meant," these people said first about a handful of issues, and then about more and more topics. Theistic evolution gained increasing approval at some evangelical colleges; evangelical feminism attracted a significant following; stewardship of God's creation all but gave way to worship of the earth in some evangelical environmental gatherings (one evangelical professor not long ago suggested to his students that lawns and sidewalks may well be outside the biblical order of things, because they are not "natural"). Homosexual practice, provided it is within a "committed and faithful monogamous relationship," now finds biblical justification by some evangelical leaders and writers—including Mr. Campolo's wife.

It's not conservatives who have hijacked the heritage of evangelicalism. It's exactly the other way around.

And simply accusing conservatives of being nothing more than me-too Republicans doesn't work either. Many of us are nearly as unhappy with secular Republicanism as we are with the agenda of the even more secular Democratic Party.

The main problem isn't which party we're connected with. The main problem is which Bible we're committed to. Shoddy exegesis, far too zealous to read outrageous new meanings into the Bible, has become the hallmark of these folks. I have no doubt they are genuine believers. But it is their own desertion of the Bible's authority that leads them now to question whether they are a legitimate part of the evangelical movement.

That's a tragic conclusion for anyone to draw. But at least when someone draws it, he ought to be ready to put the blame at the right place.

Abortion

It'll Take More Than Politics, Isaac

BY JOEL BELZ
FEBRUARY 1, 1988

MEMO TO: John Isaac Barnett

Since you had such a busy and traumatic day last week, you may not have a chance to read this for some time. I'll understand but still hope you get around to it later. The subject is important.

January 22 was a notable day for you, of course, since it was at 10:16 P.M. last Friday that you gasped your lungs full of the first air they'd ever felt.

Your entry to the world, happening when it did, came on a day of dark symbolism. I hope your future birthdays can always be happy. But you should know that they will always come on one of the saddest days on our calendar.

Always? Well, bluntly, that is what I'm writing you about. The prospects of January 22 ever being anything but a national day of mourning are not good. Even if the U.S. Supreme Court should sometime in the next half dozen years stun the nation and reverse the *Roe v. Wade* decision that exactly fifteen years before you were born opened the bloodgates of abortion, there would be nothing that could be done for the 20 million babies whose lives will already have been wasted.

Actually, Isaac, it's a statistical marvel you made it to January 22 alive. Once you had been conceived here in the United States, your chances of drawing that first breath were no better than 7 out of 10. You would have been far safer going as a marine to Vietnam. But now you have made it into this world, such as it is. Sooner than you know, it will be your task to join us in correcting those terrible odds.

And what are the odds of our doing so? Pretty grim, I think. Here's why.

Even while you've been spending the last nine months getting a bit of a head start on life, those of us on the outside world have been locked in a pretty ferocious battle having to do with who sits on that same Supreme Court that in 1973 launched the process that made your survival so chancy. It's hard to tell right now how all that might come out. But here's the point: It really might not make any difference.

We've put a lot of focus on the Supreme Court because that's where our abortion policy got so visibly off track. But the destruction brought about by that dreadful decision on your birthday in 1973 just may not be all that reversible—even if there were nine justices who wanted to do so. They would need incredible courage.

You've been born into a society, Isaac, where for better or for worse important policies are determined mostly by a majority vote. And majorities in human history have never distinguished themselves by worrying about principle. The fact is that our country has settled into a comfortable acceptance of abortion. It is an enormous convenience, and my guess is that, as a society, we'd far rather give up garbage disposals and trash compactors than our right to abortion on demand.

That's a grisly thing to tell a week-old boy. Yet it is true, Isaac, and those of us who, with your parents, will teach you what kind of world you have been born into and what God expects you to do about it, need to tell you early that the struggle will not be easy.

Both the biblical record and our own experience demonstrate that when people reject God and his standards, they are in fact choosing the way of death. Sometimes that is just a figurative way of looking at things. In the abortion debate here in the U.S., it's gone well beyond the figurative.

The battle is so much bigger than getting a 5-4 or 6-3 majority on the Supreme Court. It's bigger than getting a Human Life Amendment passed by Congress and ratified by thirty-three states. Those are important objectives, and I favor them, even though they're hard. But winning those political battles may be the easy part of your assignment. The much harder part will be to change the deep-down desires of the people the politicians represent. Don't ever kid yourself into thinking the politicians are the "bad guys" who never listen to the "basically good" people "out there." They listen, all right. The problem is that they should stop listening and start leading.

That's why this memo is to you and not to the politicians. You are the symbol of another generation. It's a long-term battle we're fighting, one that means the re-education of most of our population. It's not something that will be turned around with a few strategic votes in gold-domed buildings. It will happen instead in homes, in churches, and in classrooms where godly values begin once more to assume higher priority than personal preferences.

If it happens in your lifetime, Isaac, it will not be because of clever political strategy. It will be, as always in such cases, because God's mercy never quits.

Solomon's Decision Wouldn't Work These Days

BY JOEL BELZ
APRIL 22, 1989

It is a grisly irony that history's single great example of judicial wisdom also involved the destruction of a human baby.

That was when the two women came before King Solomon, asking him to decide which was the mother of a baby who had just died and which was the mother of the surviving infant. Solomon's reputation for wisdom rests in large measure on his memorable handling of the difficult case.

Sometime this coming week, the highest court of our land will hear arguments over what has become the most intractably divisive issue of our generation. At issue this time, however, is not just the symbolic severing of a single baby. At issue instead is our country's all-too-real mutilation and destruction of about 4,000 human babies every day of every year.

A huge difference, of course, is that King Solomon could count on the instinctive horror of a loving mother as a basis for his decision. It took no more than a hint to make the point. There never was a chance Solomon was going to use the sword he called for.

But such instincts have been hardened in our callous "civilization," and the reality of chopping up babies by the thousands is more acceptable to us than the suggestion was in Solomon's day.

Pro-abortionists argue, of course, that such images and such terminology are too vivid and too bloody and that we are sensationalizing the issue. Even an increasing number of evangelicals and should-be pro-lifers are talking that way, saying we need to "elevate" the discussion and talk about principles rather than emotions.

Meanwhile, of course, the pro-abortionists have raised the profile of their own imagery. Seeking the most terrifying symbol they can find, they've gone back to the bloodied coat hanger to scare Sandra Day O'Connor and the public away from what they fear may be coming in the next year or so.

So does that put us suddenly on even ground, each side reduced to a slightly barbaric stance? Hardly.

Last week's pro-abortion demonstration in Washington went out of its way to make it appear that pro-lifers love to see women suffer, that they get some delight out of having reluctant mothers bleed to death in back alleys. In short, they tried clumsily and grotesquely to turn the tables and make it appear that pro-lifers are the ones with blood on their hands.

And we heard again that "only" 4 percent of all U.S. abortions now occur after the sixth month. Which is to say that annually "only" 50,000 babies who are so developed you could hold them in your arms are savagely ripped apart in procedures that just a generation ago we would have associated only with a barbaric people. That happens 135 times a day in the U.S.

With all the pro-abortionists' distractions and distortions floating about, let's remember this one overarching reality: All it would take to end this bitter debate is for our society to discover again what Solomon was able to assume in his day—that a mother should love her baby.

The love we so much lack is love that keeps on loving even when it's inconvenient to do so. Solomon's wise gamble was that the true mother would rather risk the awfulness of separation from her baby than to risk the baby's death. What bitter inconvenience! But the mother's love won out.

Jesus stressed in his teachings about the last days that such love would disappear and suggested that what we think of as the natural love of parents for their children would become a rare commodity.

Which means if Solomon were sitting on the U.S. Supreme Court today, he might have to think up a new argument.

The Murderer in Us All

BY JOEL BELZ
NOVEMBER 19, 1994

Strapped by their mother into their safety seats, no less.

So if that can't help two little boys feel secure, what can? And who can doubt that Michael and Alex Smith felt secure as they slipped for the last time into the restraints that were meant to protect them but that in the end must only have added to their terror? Why shouldn't they have felt snug and safe?

"Can a mother forget the baby at her breast," Isaiah asked, "and have no compassion on the child she has borne?" (Isaiah 49:15). The prophet knew how unthinkable the thought was in the minds of his readers—or in our minds three millennia and a hundred human generations later.

But we flatter ourselves. Isaiah's point was actually very different. We tend to truncate the quote from the prophet because we like to think better of ourselves than we ought. It may be comfortable to distance ourselves from the Susan Smiths of this world, but it's ultimately dishonest to do so.

For Isaiah didn't stop where I stopped. He went on with the sober reminder that even mother-love is not constant. "Though she may forget," Isaiah reminds us, "I will not forget you." Only God is faithful. All the rest of us, in the end, are Susan Smiths.

Too harsh, you say?

Not if you think Susan Smith's two trusting boys are mirror images of what had already been happening day after day, month after month, year after year throughout our grisly society. It's impossible to think about what occurred just outside Union, S.C., a couple of weeks ago without also thinking about the parallel destruction of millions of other young lives every year through abortion. It's all one piece of cloth.

Thousands of times every single day in North America, babies who enjoy the snug security of their mothers' wombs are stunned to have that warm comfort interrupted by a violence even more repugnant than Susan Smith's rolling her Mazda down the ramp into a dark lake. Of course, it's terrifying to think about deliberate death by drowning for a three-year-old or a fourteen-month-old. But how is it different in kind from death by a chemical or death by dissection for a baby just a few months younger?

We've been over that ground in this column before—but it remains disturbing, and it should get regularly more disturbing for our whole society. Morally and ethically, how are the two circumstances different?

Can a mother forget? The painful answer from Isaiah is that yes, mothers of small children can and sometimes do forfeit their God-given propensity for serving as a child's last line of defense against violence. It should be an exceptional occurrence, and Isaiah implies that in normal God-fearing cultures it is.

But ours is less and less a God-fearing culture. For the last generation we've bent over backwards to make it the norm rather than an exception for a mother to turn a chilly heart toward her own babies. When we do that, we've got no business acting surprised when we suddenly discover a Susan Smith.

Ever since the fall in the Garden of Eden, we've selfishly wanted it both ways. We've wanted to eat the forbidden fruit and still live forever. We've wanted to have it all now and have it all later. To "have your cake and eat it too" was a notion unknown before the Fall but common afterward.

Now, bluntly, we want to be able to kill our invisible babies and still pretend that we're a genteel and humane society. We want to be able to be compassionate with every woman who chooses an abortion and still shake our heads in disbelief when we hear of another Susan Smith.

But in God's scheme of things, the erasure of such boundaries isn't possible. That's why he set flaming angels at the gates to the Garden of Eden when he banished Adam and Eve. He knew how hard they would try to go back and forth between the two kingdoms. He also knew how hard we, as their fallen children, would try to do the same thing.

President Clinton tries regularly to live in both kingdoms when he says repeatedly that he wants abortion to be "safe, legal, and rare." Perhaps he is sincere in his aspiration to all three goals; almost certainly he represents an overwhelming majority of our population in those yearnings.

Even the Republican "Contract with America"—so heartily endorsed in last week's landmark elections—tries deftly to ignore the abortion issue. We all want to be able to sin safely, to do wrong and get away with it.

But then along comes Susan Smith to remind us that God is not mocked—that a society, like a person, reaps what it sows. No way can we go for twenty years officially telling our young women that their babies are human if they want them but only tissue if they don't, and then be shocked when a young mother exercises that very choice.

Across the country last week, people professed horror that Susan Smith could have been so two-faced as to act for a week like a distraught mother when she was in fact a murderer. But maybe it's really the rest of us who are the hypocrites, acting as though Susan Smith were not the product of the very value system we have so brazenly contrived.

A Stricter Pro-Life Litmus Test

BY MARVIN OLASKY
NOVEMBER 11, 1995

Almost all *World* readers probably agree with me that there is no more crucial moral issue in our society today than abortion. Most probably agree with me that it is biblically appropriate to apply a litmus test concerning abortion. But we may have some disagreement on the type of litmus test to apply.

Here are two. Judge for yourself which is tougher.

Litmus test #1: Are you for a constitutional amendment banning abortion?

Litmus test #2: a. Have you been a volunteer counselor at a local crisis pregnancy center or contributed time and/or money to an umbrella organization such as CareNet?

b. Have you adopted a child or strongly supported adoption in some other way? Have you fought racial discrimination in adoption?

c. Have you strongly promoted abstinence? Have you worked to have abstinence programs rather than condom pimping in public schools?

d. Have you gone beyond bumper sticker pronouncements and

explained the abortion issue in a way that can convince people in the mushy middle?

e. Have you defended compassionate pro-life groups against bureaucratic harassment? Have you worked to defund Planned Parenthood and other abortion providers?

Some people can pass the first litmus test but not the second; some the second but not the first. The Republican platform should not abandon the first litmus test, but given the small likelihood of passing such an amendment over the next few years, the second deserves attention.

Here's my position: Yes on a constitutional amendment against abortion. Yes on as much legislation protecting unborn children as we can get. But do not stop there. I have written two books about the history of abortion in America and have concluded that legislation does little without enforcement, and enforcement does not happen without community consensus. Law certainly influences culture, but for the most part law follows culture.

Furthermore: Be skeptical of broad pledges. Candidates should have demonstrated in action their pro-life faith over the years; but if not, get specific commitments, not just an IOU concerning a faraway amendment. While chairing a local crisis pregnancy center, I came to see volunteer counselors as great heroines of the pro-life movement. Why not see which candidates pledge to protect them? That is concrete, not an easy out for cynics.

All of this makes for difficult appraisals at times. My friend Arianna Huffington used to be a New Ager; she is making great theological strides. She is against federal funding of abortion, but for now she opposes other protective laws. She and her husband, Michael, a California senatorial candidate last year, are contributing substantially to terrific pro-life organizations such as CareNet. They are thus legally pro-choice and compassionately pro-life. Some pro-lifers would treat them as slimeballs. I will not.

It is a lot easier to stick with litmus test #1 only. The people who insist on litmus test #1 only are among the finest of God's warriors. But passing both litmus tests is best; for the 1996 presidential race, I wish we had a strong candidate who passes both. But I cannot look at either history or today's mess and say that those who fail litmus test #1 but pass test #2 are enemies of God or of unborn children.

Nor can I say that politicians who pass #1 but fail #2 deserve our support above those who fail #1 but pass #2. Who will save more babies' lives—a president who announces his support of a constitutional amendment and does nothing, or a president who does not favor an amendment but emphatically demonstrates his support for compassionate alternatives?

And what if that president also says, "I do not favor a constitutional amendment, but I believe it is immoral to pay for abortion with the tax money of pro-life Americans. I will veto any expenditure for abortion, including any federal funds for Planned Parenthood"? How many lives will be saved if that evil empire takes a $100 million hit?

The Bible is clear: Abortion is murder. But the best way to save millions of children's lives, in this Babylon of a culture where God's providence has placed us, is not always so clear. We need to love the Lord not only with our hearts and souls but also with our minds.

Building Pro-Life Alliances

BY MARVIN OLASKY
JANUARY 13, 1996

A current pizza chain commercial features Dallas Cowboys owner Jerry Jones asking one of his well-paid stars, Deion Sanders, whether he wants to play offense or defense, whether he wants one multimillion-dollar contract or another, and whether he wants one type of pizza or another. Sanders's answer is always, "Both."

That should be the answer of pro-lifers when faced with the repeated questions about whether our movement should concentrate on culture or politics, on providing compassionate alternatives to abortion or changing laws, on influencing the elite or working at the grass roots. And that answer should carry with it a refusal to turn against friends such as Bill Bennett who are with us on some pro-life tasks but not on others.

The pro-life movement during 1995 reversed the mushrooming malaise of 1993 and 1994 and showed some pepperoni. One spark was political: Success in electing many new pro-life members of Congress led to debate and passage of a bill opposing one of the most grotesque forms of abortion. Another spark was cultural: the conversion of Norma McCorvey, the "Roe" of *Roe v. Wade.*

Congressional debate and Christ's mercy reminded some magazine editors that the abortion debate is still with us and provoked some writers into reconsidering and further refining their positions. The articles that emerged in magazines such as *The New Republic, Atlantic,* and *The Weekly Standard* will provoke readers to further thought and action.

And meanwhile, volunteers at crisis pregnancy centers throughout the country continued to wrestle with the consciences of unmarried pregnant women, praying throughout the night that they will receive a blessing at dawn and witness morning in America once more.

The events of 1995 showed once again that law and culture, politics and education are interconnected. The law is a teacher, and so is the process of passing laws or pushing for constitutional amendments. Providentially, the requirements for passage of an amendment—two-thirds of the House and Senate and three-fourths of the state legislatures—force those who want change on a controversial issue to develop broad support.

The Republican platform should not drop the hope for a constitutional amendment because it will be difficult to attain one; that is precisely the reason the goal should be retained. An amendment should be seen not as a prize to be won through a Beltway coup, but as the logical outgrowth of a successful culture-winning strategy. Just because a generation-long educational process will be needed is no reason to shirk from it, nor to use the long, slow task as an excuse to do little now.

Cynical politicians can use vague support for a constitutional amendment as such an excuse, however. For that reason, Republican candidates in each state during 1996 should be pushed to commit themselves to achievable legislative action in 1997 that would provide some immediate help: waiting periods, parental consent, a ban on third-trimester abortions, defunding of Planned Parenthood and other abortion providers, and protection of pro-life counseling centers from regulatory counterattack. The party platform should deal with both the long-term goal and the immediately achievable.

Divisiveness in the pro-life movement can stop progress, however. Advocates of the cultural approach should support good legislation, and political partisans should not think of the "compassionate alternative" advocates as weak sisters. The two sides help each other as they compete for effectiveness in a way that is win-win rather than zero-sum.

All of us need to remember that the abortionists' evil empire can fall as the Soviet Union did, but years of containment may still be necessary. During those years God will not be silent. One of my heroes, Whittaker Chambers, dated his initial break with communism to the time his young daughter smeared porridge on her face. Chambers found himself looking at her "intricate, perfect ears." He saw immense design, not a chance coming together of atoms—and "at that moment, the finger of God was first laid upon my forehead."

God's finger is touching many foreheads now. He is also using a variety of human means—politics, education, culture, personal crisis—to place in the minds of millions of Americans an image of an intricately made unborn child. As that portrait made not by human hands overwhelms murderous rationalizations, God's finger will write on the walls of the abortionists' dining halls that their days are numbered.

Adoption: Safe, Legal, and Sadly Rare

BY MARVIN OLASKY
JANUARY 27, 1996

Life under secular liberalism does not make sense. Millions of "unwanted" unborn children have been murdered on grounds that are not only ethically unjustifiable but factually incorrect, since so many parents desperately want those children.

The adoption situation is so crazy that many people, including pro-lifers, give up on it and marginalize adoption by thinking of it as a good thing but, in massive quantities, practically unachievable. That defeatism must be fought, because we will not be able to take a big bite out of abortion unless adoption becomes central in pro-life thinking once more.

Here's why: While the vast majority of Americans know that abortion is the killing of a human being, many view abortion as justifiable homicide, self-defense against tiny intruders who will ruin the lives of young women unless they are (with regrets) snuffed out. Pro-lifers need to realize that the big battle is no longer whether unborn children have beating hearts. That battle, wonderfully, is largely won. The big battle is whether killing unborn children is murder or justifiable homicide.

Those who take the Bible seriously know that abortion is in no way justifiable. Secularists, though, need to be shown that unmarried pregnant women without recourse to marriage have an alternative to either committing homicide against their unborn children or suffering the life imprisonment of an impoverished single parenthood.

The alternative offered by government over the past generation has been a welfare system that creates slightly less impoverishment among beneficiaries in the short term, while building a culture of irresponsibility that creates more poverty over time. Just as abortion has benefited from federal laws and court rulings that give it special protection, so welfare has flourished as eighty different federal programs give its takers special funding.

Now, roughly 49 percent of unmarried pregnant women grab hold of abortion, 49 percent skip into single-parenting, and only 2 percent choose adoption, the alternative that offers little support and significant legal uncertainties. Now, for many pregnant and unmarried teens, abortion seems to convey an immediate benefit: Make the problem disappear. (And don't worry about death or post-abortion regrets that grow more severe as time goes by.)

Now, single-parenting conveys benefits: Love from a child and money from the only rich uncle (Sam) some kids know. Now, adoption is merely altruistic—life for a child and a gift to an often-childless couple. Teenagers generally do not ask what they can do for others. Adoption is safe, legal, but rare.

Many welfare programs, despite their unpopularity, have survived as a way to make the hard task of single-parenting slightly less so. Even some pro-lifers have supported what they know is a bad alternative, welfare, out of fear that otherwise the worse alternative, abortion, will become even more common. But that is lesser-of-two-evils pragmatism run amuck.

The lesser of two evils can be reluctantly but rightly chosen in circumstances (as in a political race) where such a position points us in the right direction. A continued embrace of the welfare state, however, points to the destruction of one of the major blessings, family, that God has given us. The goal should be to replace federal AFDC with community-based programs that include maximum efforts to promote marriage and adoption, so every child can have both a father and a mother.

Some inner-city churches are emphasizing marriage more strongly now, and some Christian social agencies are finding practical ways to make the blessings of a two-parent family available to more children through adoption. For example, in Kansas City the Lighthouse maternity home has mandatory classes on both adoption and child-rearing, so young women can make an informed choice. Some 40 percent of the babies born there since the home opened in 1985—that's 230 out of 575—have been placed for adoption.

Pro-lifers who understand that the federal government should not enshrine the worst choice, abortion, as a fundamental legal right should move on to stop government enshrinement of the mediocre choice, single-parenting, as a fundamental economic right. Instead of pouring money into welfare programs that create more heat, we should back development of lighthouse alternatives.

Such programs will transform lives and change minds. As adoption becomes common, those in the mushy middle will find it harder and harder to justify homicide. By promoting adoption we can eventually gain a life-protecting constitutional amendment because the constitution of American thought will have changed.

Government

The $1 Checkoff

BY JOEL BELZ
APRIL 28, 1990

Conventional wisdom says that you should watch out for the person who tells little fibs even when he doesn't have to. That's the guy, experience shows, who will later take you to the cleaners with some really big-time embezzlement or theft.

I thought of that last week as I was finishing up my taxes and pondered how it applies to the federal government.

The two-line promise near the top of your tax form that says that if you designate $1 for the next presidential election campaign, you won't have to worry that your tax bill will be any higher than if you didn't designate the dollar—that promise is false on the face of it.

Clearly, if the federal government spends $100 million for an election campaign, which it does every four years, that money has to come from somewhere. The promise on the tax form implies that the $100 million appears out of thin air. But in fact the money comes, just like every other dollar the government spends, from taxpayers like you and me.

So even if you didn't technically have to add $1 to this year's tax bill, you can rest assured that same dollar will be part of next year's bite. It has to be.

Clearly, the issue here is not so much the 10 cents a year such a policy extracts from every man, woman, and child in the country. As broke as we are, we can probably afford that.

What we can't afford is the pretense. A government willing to lie to its citizens about a small amount like that ought to understand the anger of its citizens when they discover they've also been lied to about Social Security and about a savings and loan scandal that will cost not just a dime a year, but thousands of dollars per citizen. The same government talks glibly about the regulations it imposes on us all while barely mentioning the dollars-and-cents, year-in-and-year-out costs such regulations bring with them.

So then we have to ask: If they fibbed to us about the $1 on the tax form, and lied to us about Social Security and the savings and loans losses, why do we trust them on any of the other really big issues?

If fiscal ruin comes, it won't be primarily because economic conservatives or liberals were at the helm and made a few wrong decisions while fine-tuning the economy. It will come instead because moral ruin took over just a few years earlier.

God's Law Library

BY JOEL BELZ
NOVEMBER 3, 1990

The failure of the so-called civil rights bill of 1990 was a reminder of how differently God and men go about crafting the laws by which they expect other people to live.

God's rules tend to be simple, few, non-contradictory, and sufficient to stand the test of time without constant updating.

Man's laws—even when they're well-intended, like the civil rights bill may have been—are complex, lengthy, repetitive, full of contradictions, and constantly in need of revision and amendment.

Nor is this just another swipe at the federal government. The contrast between God's approach and man's approach to writing rules is just as evident when you look at the bylaws of your local church or the constitution of a PTA or a garden club. We're just not very good at anticipating all the needs and the eventualities that our weak human natures will give rise to. Just as soon as we think we have everything nailed down, somebody's sinful inventiveness finds another loophole—and we have to come up with a new bill or another list of amendments.

A major reason for this difference may be that, unlike God, we have limited power and look to the law as a means of controlling other people's behavior. God, meanwhile, uses his law not so much to control us (which he does anyway) as he does to teach us his wisdom.

That's why he started, early in the Bible, by expressing his desires for our behavior in ten brief, broad strokes. Any one of them had a thousand implications, but part of his wisdom was not to spell all that out with subtopics, footnotes, or a complicated decimal system. Instead, he left it simple—and memorable.

That, incidentally, is one of the great benefits of brevity. People can remember what you say. The shame of our day, even in evangelical circles, is that so few people have taken time to memorize the Ten Commandments. But it is altogether possible, even easy, to do. And that is no accident on God's part; he made it easy because "he knows our frame; he remembers that we are dust" (Psalm 103:14, KJV).

God starts with profound simplicity rather than with multi-volume legal codes because he wants us to apply our hearts to the task of wisdom, not rote obedience. Yes, it's true he wants compliance. But he could have that anytime he desires it. What he wants even more is for our remade hearts to think their way through and then to desire fervently the way of life he has designed for us. There's no legal library anywhere in the world with shelves long enough for all the books it would take to spell out in detail so rich a code.

So he gives us instead ten brief and clear starting points. If we incline our hearts in his direction, those ten points blossom out into a hundred new challenges we never thought of before; but obedience up-front then makes it amazingly less complicated to understand the subsequent challenges and far less difficult to obey them. Only when we stubbornly turn the other direction at the starting point do matters get complicated and difficult.

Prudent parents want exactly the same thing as they work to bring their children to wisdom and maturity. They don't want those youngsters to carry around a burdensome code book of rules the rest of their lives. Instead, they seek to have them adopt as their own a few important principles from which wise decisions can spontaneously flow as each challenge or temptation arises.

Those who fashion civil law should consider such wisdom as an appropriate goal for citizens of the state as well. There's a big difference, for example, between God's simple formula for figuring the tithe on the one hand and IRS's interminable rules and regulations on the other. What would happen if the tax moguls scrapped the whole system now in force and made the process as simple as God's is?

Maybe IRS isn't the place to begin. But wherever they start, Congress and the Washington bureaucracy had better come to understand pretty soon that however much they may think they're refining the process, the production of stacks and stacks of regulations actually breeds contempt for the law. It's tough to obey what you have no chance of comprehending. And even if you do manage some sort of technical compliance, it usually isn't from the heart.

God Didn't Delegate the Decalogue to Congress

BY JOEL BELZ
NOVEMBER 9, 1991

Get down on your knees right now and thank God that the U.S. Congress had nothing to do with writing the Ten Commandments. You'd never understand God's law if they had.

I had made up my mind to oppose the Civil Rights Act of 1991 even before I read the text of the legislation. Then, while in Washington last week, I thought how intellectually dishonest that was; certainly I owed it to the drafters of the bill and those in Congress who were pushing it at least to know what it said.

So we chased down a copy of the bill (even that is harder than you might think) and sat down to read it. If it had been the tablets from Mount Sinai, this is roughly how Stone No. 1 would have read:

SEC. 1. SHORT TITLE. This act may be cited as "The Ten Commandments."

SEC. 2. FINDINGS. The Congress finds that—

(1) additional remedies under Israeli law are needed to deter unlawful attitudes and behavior toward God and man.

(2) actions of the leader Moses relating to the fight between two Hebrews demonstrated the inability of citizens to know clearly God's preferences in such circumstances.

(3) extensive public discourse notwithstanding, "natural law" has proven itself an inadequate revelation of the details of God's desires for his people.

SEC. 3. PURPOSES. The purposes of this act are—

(1) to provide appropriate remedies for intentional or unintentional breaches of the standards of God.

(2) to codify the concept of "loving God with all your heart" and "loving your neighbor as yourself."

(3) to confirm statutory authority and provide statutory guidelines for the adjudication of . . .

Still with me? What you just read is roughly a one-for-one translation of the actual Civil Rights Act of 1991 as applied to the Ten Commandments. The huge difference is this: The whole text of the Ten Commandments is just 298 words long. What you just read is already more than half of that—and yet it is only 4 percent of the whole Civil Rights Act. If we reprinted the whole bill here, it would go on for five more pages of solid type in this format—with no pictures. Not included here are Sections 4 through 22, which spell out definitions, clarifications, damages, determinations, limitations, constructions, prohibitions, facilitations, resolutions, exemptions, applications, challenges, presumptions, protections, expansions, authorizations, and so many other provisions that the average citizen cannot possibly know whether or how to comply with the law.

I know I'm in trouble—and so is all of American society—as soon as I read a passage like this: "Section 703 of the Civil Rights Act of 1964 (42 U.S.C. 2000e-2) is amended by adding at the end of the following new subsection: (k)(1)(A) an unlawful employment practice based on disparate impact is established under this title only if— . . ." If I'm discouraged from comprehending what's expected of me, how can I possibly obey any law?

And what about a small business like God's World Publications Inc., with a few more than twenty full-time and about forty more part-time employees? No way can we afford a staff of specialists to tell us whether or not we're in compliance. It's not a matter of trying to get by. It has simply to do with basic appreciation of what's expected of us as citizens.

So now I'm back where I started—except that having read the Civil
Rights Act of 1991 (twice, as a matter of fact) I'm more against it than
before I read it. Laws that are unintelligible to the people who must live
under them—no matter how well intentioned—are counterproductive.
Instead of inspiring citizens to moral behavior, such laws stimulate base
cynicism among us all.

You might hear some complaints here and there about the Ten
Commandments. One complaint you'll never hear, though, is that folks
just don't understand what they mean.

Real Compassion Is Costly

BY JOEL BELZ
FEBRUARY 26, 1994

Compassion that is not costly to its giver is ultimately no compassion at
all. Love that does not lose something for its donor is not the deepest kind
of love.

Those truths, rooted in the Scripture, also have much to do with the
fact that big government can never adequately perform some of the func-
tions in life we have come to expect from it in modern society. Take three
examples: education, medical care, and old-age care. If anything should
be apparent, it is that those three needs in life ought to be swathed in all
the wrappings of intimacy we can muster.

Simply to ask, then, whether big government can provide such intimacy is to provide the answer.

A "loving government" isn't just an oxymoron. It's something that
can't be just by its very nature. A government has nothing of its own to
give. Everything it has it gets from others—and that by force of law. So
there is no way that it, as government, can sacrifice.

Parents can sacrifice. They can sit up and rock an infant when they'd
rather sleep. They can skip a vacation trip to pay for braces. They can work
an extra job to help make college possible.

Teachers can sacrifice. They can stay with you after school to help
with long division. They can work all day Saturday on a class fund-

raiser. They can explain things a little when your girlfriend breaks up with you.

Doctors and nurses can sacrifice. They can meet you at 1 A.M. to stitch a lacerated chin. Your pediatrician can hang a sign on his office door that says "GONE TO GHANA TO HELP THE CHILDREN THERE" (as ours used to do once a year or so) and thus leave a profound message with your own children.

Even families can sacrifice. They can double up in their own rooms to free one for Grandpa who just had a stroke and isn't his old self but would die an early death if put in a nursing home. They can adjust their daily schedules to make loving room for a sometimes hard-to-understand oldster.

But oddly, governments can't sacrifice. All governments can ever do is fake their compassion—because the compassion of a big government costs it nothing at all. In the name of compassion, the U.S. Congress over the next few months will pretend it is really concerned with the health care of millions of Americans. Yet it will do so primarily by raising taxes for the rest of us. Meanwhile, members of Congress will quietly continue to make their own health claims on an insurance program set up just for them and other branches of the federal government. There's no pain at all for them in their do-goodism—neither in paying for the system they will foist on us nor in living under it themselves. The only thing such a system has in common with compassion is that the word *cynical* also starts with the letter *c*.

In fact, the contrast between a sacrificing parent and cynical Congress suggests this rule of thumb: the farther you move from the individual orbit toward the big group, the harder it is to engage in genuine sacrifice. For almost as soon as we start assembling ourselves in bigger and bigger groups, we also start engaging in various kinds of "risk aversion." Discomforts we were quite ready to endure when we were alone now must regularly and studiously be avoided.

Examples abound. Little churches do their own janitorial work on a volunteer basis; megachurches hire sanitary engineering companies. Teachers in one-room schools put Band-Aids on the students themselves; teachers in big schools have to send kids to the infirmary. Bosses in little companies regularly do things with and for their employees that they tend to quit doing when the payroll extends to hundreds of people.

Bigness, all by itself—not just in government, but anywhere—tends to discourage sacrificial behavior. That happens for a very simple reason. Only individuals, or at best small groups of individuals, actually have the resources needed to engage in sacrifice. You can't sacrifice that which you don't own in the first place.

But it isn't enough just to beat up on government and other big entities for trying to do what by their very nature they're not equipped to do. Instead, we desperately need to get busy doing those thing ourselves. If the God-intended model is for persons, not super-agencies, to wrap their arms around little children and patients and aging parents, then the only way to implement that model is to do it person by person. Certainly it won't be implemented by having big agencies mandate such involvement by individuals.

To be sure, there are those who complain that they'd love to get involved in such compassionate activities except that the government got there first and is in the way. Or we complain that the government has so drained our resources that we have nothing left to work with ourselves.

There is substance in those excuses—but they are still excuses. The very nature of sacrifice means that you're so consumed with the opportunity for service that you can't even see or feel the hindrances.

A New Battle at the Alamo

BY MARVIN OLASKY
JULY 29, 1995

In front of the Alamo on July 17, 100 signs that should wake up even hardened government officials shone in the noonday sun. Typical messages on the signs read: "Because of Jesus I Am No Longer a Debt to the State of Texas" and "Once a Burden, Now a Taxpayer." The astounding response from the Texas state government? To continue its efforts to harass Teen Challenge of South Texas, the program that has produced such successes.

Unusual? No. TCADA, the Texas Commission on Alcohol and Drug Abuse, and its counterparts in other states have for three decades stomped on privately-funded, Bible-based, anti-addiction programs. But last week's enthusiastic rally—with the temperature in the mid-90s, 325 persons stood for two hours to hear heated, socially conservative rhetoric and sing "When the Saints Go Marching In"—shows that the political dynamic may be changing.

There's no denying that TCADA has a case against Teen Challenge, which argues that the root cause of alcoholism and addiction is "man's separation from God. . . . Sinful behavior, including compulsive deviant behavior, is engaged in to fill the void of meaninglessness in life." Teen Challenge groups around the country have successfully fought substance abuse since 1958 by teaching that life has God-given meaning beyond drugs and that each person has God-given potential that he should use. The state agency sniffs at such logic and complains that "no substance abuse treatment, as defined by TCADA standards, is given."

There's also no denying that state inspectors get the willies when they observe Teen Challenge's hiring (often former addicts and alcoholics who had their own lives turned around by the program), paper-minimalism (violation of standard 116a, which requires each personnel file to have nine specific sets of records, and standard 144b, which requires a formal, six-step client grievance procedure), and make-do tendencies in the absence of government funding (violation of standard 353h: Stairs are supposed to have uniform "non-slip surfaces," but on Teen Challenge stairs "Some carpeting edges need repair").

But compare all that with the records of lives changed. At the Alamo rally the brief testimonies kept coming. One grizzled man said, "I was a junkie in the streets of San Antonio for thirteen years. I was a thief. I went to the government programs. They didn't work. Jesus set me free." A pretty woman in her twenties recalled, "When I was a hooker the Christians would come and talk to me; I'd blow smoke in their faces, but I was sort of listening. Then I came and learned." A brawny guy held a Bible and told how, when he was fourteen, "My dad said, 'I'm gonna show you how to be a man,' so he tied my arm and showed me how to shoot heroin. Then we were in the pen, and he'd point me out to other prisoners and say, 'That's my boy, he's just like me.' Now we both know Jesus, and we're clean."

It was hot outside but cool inside the Alamo itself, cool and hushed. After all, the Alamo was a mission, and now it's a secular church with shrine rules of quiet. Some people stood before one of the wall plaques— Colonel Travis's "Letter to the People of Texas and all Americans in the World"—reading the words silently, sometimes moving their lips: "I call on you in the name of liberty, of patriotism & everything dear to the American character to come to our aid, with all dispatch. . . . P.S. The Lord is on our side."

Outside, in the heat, pleas for help continued: "Teen Challenge isn't being closed down because it's ineffective, but because it works. It is a threat to the whole poverty industry. These people who are trying to take Teen Challenge's license: Where were they when I needed help?" And where are Christians from across America now that Teen Challenge needs help? The speakers at the rally were in essence penning a new letter to the People of Texas, to all Americans, and especially to all Christians: "Come to our aid, with all dispatch. P.S. The Lord is on our side."

A Deceptively Simple List

BY JOEL BELZ
FEBRUARY 17, 1996

The advent of the television V-chip, and its sudden popularity among so many politicians, proves that conservatives are way too much like liberals. We all have an overweening fix-it mentality. Evangelical Christians included, we get carried away with our sense that every problem in life has a publicly sponsored solution.

The V-chip, mandated almost without dissent a few days ago in a House of Representatives telecommunications bill, is supposedly designed to give parents the ability to block out certain television programming from their children's viewing schedules. If approved by both the Senate and President Clinton, V-chips will by law be required on all new TV sets.

As with so many well-intentioned laws, people will probably feel a wee bit safer. In fact, they should know just how much more vulnerable they have made themselves.

Relying on the V-chip, in fact, is a little like fastening your seat belt, glancing confidently at your air bag, and then mashing the accelerator and zinging yourself 30 mph past the speed limit. The safety devices might help in an isolated case—but that's a horrible way to control accidents.

What's needed instead are sane and sensible people behind the wheel.

That, indeed, is what is needed through all of society. The law is poor enough at changing people's behavior; it's all but hopeless to use it to change people's hearts.

But wait! Isn't that precisely the line of reasoning the pro-abortion lobby uses all the time to argue against laws restricting abortion? Yes— and that's what gets us back to the main topic here: Some issues take precedence over others, and not all urges to pass a law are created equal.

The signers of the Declaration of Independence understood that a good bit better than we tend to today. When they spelled out the benefits that a government ought to seek to provide for its citizens, our forebears pointed to (1) life, (2) liberty, and (3) the pursuit of happiness. It's a deceptively simple list, but profoundly limited and just as profoundly sequenced.

The protection and defense of life heads the list of proper governmental responsibilities. Other threats might have to be interpreted, negotiated, waited out, or even winked at. But life itself is so important in God's scheme of things that he made it the reward for perfect obedience by human beings, while imposing life's opposite—death—as the ultimate penalty for disobedience. No one trifles with this great gift of God without suffering terrible consequences. Whether it's big armies wreaking havoc with whole populations, gangs doing drive-by shootings, or doctors callously aborting babies, governments have not just a right but a responsibility to get involved big-time in stopping such killing.

Not far behind the obligation to protect life is the duty to safeguard the liberty of the living. Indeed, both life and liberty are primary derivatives of being made in the image of God. To allow a person life but not liberty is constantly to mock the life itself. Yet neither dare we forget that the priority is life first, then liberty; for my liberty is always bounded by another person's right to live. But it is altogether right for governments to see the protection of liberty, for both individuals and classes of individuals, as a high duty.

Only third on the list of the things a government should seek for its citizens—after life and liberty—comes the more general quality of happiness. Well, no, not really. For the writers of the Declaration had the good sense to understand that no government either is or even ought to be so powerful as to pretend it can make all its citizens happy. The best it really can do is to order circumstances so that people can pursue that happiness on their own.

So the list and its order are remarkably instructive. They explain why the military is a legitimate preoccupation of government, why a prohibition of abortion is an altogether right thing to legislate, and why a government has a duty to take strong steps to ensure that black people who have never voted before feel free to do so.

But the list also explains why a federal government should refrain from micro-managing the moral content of television. No matter how desirable the immediate result of such micro-management might be, we're simply looking to the wrong agent when we ask a big, cumbersome, awkward (and very secular) agent to help bring it about.

Sociologist Glenn Loury was pointed in his recent comment to host Ken Myers of Mars Hill Tapes: "Conservative social engineering is no prettier, in my judgment, than liberal social engineering. The human being is not a mechanism. [No one] understands the depths of the human heart. There's a certain arrogant presumption that [the liberals'] game plan was wrong, but now we've got the right game plan. Let's lay it down and fix America."

Concentrate on life. Concentrate on liberty. But nine times out of ten, vote against legislation that tries to order human behavior on just about any other issue.

Back to Basics for the Government

BY MARVIN OLASKY
APRIL 20, 1996

While the Freemen tie themselves down in their Montana fort, slaves in other places try to escape. Frequently a call from a Los Angeles teenage hooker locked in a hotel room comes to the Children of the Night switchboard. Typical message: Her pimp has beaten her and threatens to do worse. She wants out. How can she escape?

The phone counselor is trained to respond quickly: "Give us your exact address. We can have a black and white [a Los Angeles police car] come to that room within five minutes. Do you want the cops to pretend to arrest you? That'll get you out safely."

This is standard operating procedure to Lois Lee, president of

Children of the Night, an organization based in L.A. that runs a nation-wide hotline and a shelter for teens escaping from prostitution. She knows how to get help from the government: "When we call the police, we ask the person at the front desk to connect us with the watch commander. The people at the front desk are there because they're not competent. But others are. They move quickly."

Mrs. Lee wants the government to move quickly to prosecute the marketers of sexual exploitation. She wants the government to protect her shelter from enraged pimps attempting midnight reclamations of their teenaged meal tickets: "The police can have a copter in the air shining lights down on us in five minutes." She wants the police to help her keep the shelter drug-free: "The LAPD brings its drug-sniffing dogs over for training exercises. If there's been any drugs in a dresser during the past two weeks, dogs will sniff it."

Mrs. Lee has seen how the government can help. She also saw in 1992, when her shelter opened, how the government can hurt: "Regulations were a problem: They wanted us to have handicapped-access rooms. I told them that all the kids here were prostitutes, they don't need handicapped rooms. Kids in wheelchairs carry dope."

Mrs. Lee's logic was impeccable, but the government was unmovable. She finally agreed to put in a ramp that would connect one door to a yard area. (To this day, it never has been used.) But there was more: Until the ramp actually was in place, she had to agree that no one would ever open that particular door to go into the yard.

She promised that if a handicapped teenage prostitute were to show up, the young woman and her wheelchair would be carried down the three steps. No, officials insisted, no one can go out that door—and they had their way.

The Los Angeles rampists were not singling out Children of the Night for special treatment; idiocy seems to be standard operating procedure. In 1994 a city commission forced a striptease joint to close a "shower stall" on its stage because the stall would not be accessible to strippers in wheelchairs, were there to be such.

Children of the Night's travails did not end with the closed-door-until-ramp-arrives policy. The shelter was ready for occupancy, and teens were waiting to enter, but a licensing official did not show up for a final inspection. Not until Mrs. Lee scheduled an opening day for the center and told the official, "I will hate to tell the press that we can't open because you won't come" did the inspector come and give her blessing.

Government can do some things well: Lois Lee has used the police to insure domestic tranquillity. She has also seen government make charitable organizations jump through its hoops. A *Los Angeles Times* article in 1981, just as Mrs. Lee was getting started, reported that "Children of the Night typically shuns government money because, in the words of Lee, 'there are not strings, but ropes attached to state and federal funds.' She argues that with smaller amounts from private individuals the integrity of the program can be preserved, and administrative costs will remain small." A decade and a half later, the same logic applies.

We should apply Lois Lee's experience with government help and government hindrance to our political understanding. The Freemen of Montana are anti-government, but truly free citizens should be more discerning. Our problem is not just that we have too much government, but that we have not enough of the right kind—firm and fair use of the biblically-approved power of the sword. The Bible and the Constitution give civil government some carefully defined powers, with a particular emphasis placed on preserving law and order. Let's stick to that, vote out the power-coveters who favor government controls in other areas, and cut out the mischief.

Where Have You Gone, Joe Democracy?

BY MARVIN OLASKY
MAY 11, 1996

One of my favorite historians is Claude Bowers, an Indiana journalist who was born in 1878 and moonlighted during the 1920s and 1930s by writing evocative books about Jefferson, Jackson, and the Reconstruction period. Mr. Bowers was also a noted political speaker who gave keynote addresses and key nominating speeches at Democratic Party conventions in the 1920s.

Democrat? Readers who know that I'm most often identified these days with the Republican side of things might wonder about my preference for a political activist on the other side. But one reason I like Bowers is that he was not on the other side. He was a Democrat when that party opposed increases in centralized power and fought for middle-class America. He was a conservative Democrat who was then in the mainstream of a party that respected and tried to protect families, churches, and small businesses.

Bowers would have no place in today's party, however. Democrats now make noises about limiting government but can't beat their addiction to taxing and spending. President Clinton proclaimed in his 1996 State of the Union address, "The era of big government is over" and then made an initial request to the returning Congress: $8 billion more in new spending for the current fiscal year. His fiscal year 1997 budget offered a $358 billion increase over the levels proposed in Congress' seven-year balanced budget plans.

There's something deeper than budgetary dishonesty going on here. Serious moral errors infect the liberalism that is at the core of the modern Democratic Party. Professor J. Budziszewski, a colleague of mine at the University of Texas, noted seven of them in the March issue of the journal *First Things*. Among the moral errors are perfectionism, the doctrine that human effort is adequate to cure human evil, and neutralism, the notion that we should become tolerant by suspending judgments about good or evil.

Perfectionism, of course, makes God's grace unnecessary, and neutralism makes God himself boorish for insisting that we should discern good from evil and then fight for the good. The liberals who now dominate the Democrats talk neutralism ("all cultures are equal") and in practice undermine God-given institutions such as family and church. They see these institutions as inhibiting the drive to a free, uninhibited, perfect humanity.

Republicans often portray today's Democratic Party as an assemblage of dollar-seeking interest groups with elegant public relations names such as the Children's Defense Fund, Planned Parenthood, and the National Education Association—but that's only half the story. Washington reporters (89 percent of whom voted for Bill Clinton in 1992, according to a recent survey) complain about the religious right, but the White House and federal courts still promote the sacraments of the religious left, including abortion, radical feminism, and the welfare state.

The brawling Democratic Party of Bowers's era has become a cult that shuns those who do not embrace each of its doctrines. In 1992 Bob

Casey, then governor of Pennsylvania and a staunch Democrat in every area but one, wanted to present a pro-life message at the party convention; he was told that no dissenting voices were allowed. It's all very sad, because the Democratic Party had great debates for over a century before it became a party of national elites and the government-dependent.

There is one continuity between the old Democratic Party and the new: each made or makes its peace with racism. The old party, with its solid South base, demanded preferences for whites; the new party, with its solid African-American base, demands preferences for blacks. Both bigotries were, are, and ever will be wrong. If the Democratic Party became color-blind and at the same time opened its eyes to the evil of abortion and the folly of big government spending, it could draw back into it millions of Bowers Democrats.

And maybe donkeys will fly. Why even contemplate such an unlikely notion? The reason is that political parties change; keeping one moving in lockstep for very long is like stuffing a live octopus into a string bag and expecting that none of the arms will hang out. At this moment Democrats are optimistic, but only a year ago, reeling from their 1994 electoral whomping, some rethinking of mission was occurring.

Political trends may again change before the end of the century; if they do, Claude Bowers could become must reading, and a Simon and Garfunkel tune, with new lyrics, could be more than a mournful dirge. Let's sing it together: "Where have you gone, Joe Democracy? A nation turns its lonely eyes to you."

The Supreme Court and Prayer: Only Two Things Can Happen—Both Bad

BY JOEL BELZ
NOVEMBER 16, 1991

Only two things are likely to happen as a result of the Supreme Court's renewed interest in the matter of praying in public places such as high school graduations and college football games. Both of them are bad.

The first is that the Court will maintain the perverted judgment it has forwarded during the past generation that such prayer is wrong. To allow such prayer, the Court has preached for nearly thirty years, is to allow the establishment of religion in precisely the manner that the U.S. Constitution forbids. But in pushing that argument, the Court so badly misinterprets and overstates what the Constitution actually says that it ends up blatantly restricting the freedoms guaranteed in the same clause of the First Amendment. Why not use the same tortured reasoning to forbid any travel on an interstate highway that enables someone to drive to a prayer meeting? Such a prohibition would make just as much sense.

The other bad thing that might come from the Supreme Court's hearing of the prayer issue, however, is that it might decide to begin allowing a little bit of prayer. Not what the Bible calls prayer, mind you, or what Jehovah God calls prayer. There's little chance of anything that fervent getting the approval even of a newly conservative Supreme Court. But it's altogether possible Rehnquist & Co. will put their imprimatur on something "nonsectarian and inoffensive."

For Christians, that might be even worse than no prayer at all. On balance, if we have to choose between no prayer and prayer so sterilized we can't pour our hearts out to God or call him by the name he tells us to use, then we shouldn't kid ourselves into thinking we're praying at all. Nor should we let any court—even a conservative one—encourage us in such pretense.

The real solution is two-fold. First, we need to take the Constitution literally. Those actions that are proscribed are only the ones that actually help establish an organized religion as a function of the state. Second, we should reduce the number of contexts in which the state sponsors public events. If the state ran no schools, for example, 95 percent of the question about state-sponsored praying would immediately disappear.

Education

Archimedes Was Right

BY JOEL BELZ
FEBRUARY 10, 1990

The great battle waiting for biblical Christians over the coming decade, and probably over the next generation or two, is not over abortion or pornography or racism or free enterprise or justice for the poor—or even inerrancy.

The great battle is over who has the right, and the freedom, to educate our children. All the other issues will more or less fall in line if we get that one right.

Archimedes was on target when he observed, "Give me where to stand, and I will move the earth." But the opposite is also true: Take away your footing, and you'll not be able to move anything at all.

There are two ways to take away a person's most essential footing. One is to replace that footing with error. The other is to replace it with thin air. Under state sponsorship of education, the children of Christ's kingdom have been subjected to both approaches—and we should be terrified by the prospect of what lies in store for them as a result. On a whole variety of issues, their ability to think or act significantly has been neutered.

We could recite here the almost unending catalog of outright error offered under state auspices in subjects such as science, history, social studies, and literature. But that is not the main point.

Much more telling are the millions of evangelical children who are regularly told that what they believe is OK, of course—but that what everyone else believes is OK too. In such a system, the main article of faith is that everyone's faith is as good as anyone else's. That's what we mean when we talk about offering a foundation of thin air. It's not the kind of foundation where world-movers like to stand.

But it is the foundation that the state in this part of history is virtually obliged to offer. The state cannot even approach telling the truth, the whole truth, and nothing but the truth—at least insofar as the truth is understood by Christians. So it has made itself comfortable assuring children that all truth is relative. That has worked surprisingly well, considering how skinny and wimpy the doctrine really is.

In fact, it has worked so well on every level, from kindergarten through the college and university level, that the pressure is on now to apply the same philosophy to preschool children. Without a terrific outcry from hundreds of thousands of concerned people, that is precisely what is likely to happen sometime in 1990.

The result, of course, will put just that many more American children in double jeopardy. I say double jeopardy because the record is clear that those who buy into such a system end up short-changed not just philosophically but also in terms of their basic competencies. You cannot mock God on one end of the level and expect to see an improvement in your SAT scores on the other end.

All this would be sobering enough if our only challenge were to remind Christians what their personal risks and choices are. But when, as is the case with the day-care issue, the state raises the ante by threatening to rape our very young, just as it already has our elementary, secondary, and college youth, those risks become higher and the choices that much more precious.

Another whole chunk of ground, where we used to have a little footing, is being shoveled away. The task of moving the world will be just that much harder.

McDonald's Without McGuffey?

BY JOEL BELZ
APRIL 7, 1990

Imagine that you're the manager of a local McDonald's restaurant. For the third straight day, as you close out your registers your cash record is off.

But now, as you reflect on what might be happening and think about the various members of your youthful staff, you puzzle over a strange pair of possible explanations. Are you dealing with computational incompetence or with day-to-day dishonesty?

For you, and for thousands of other employers like you, the answer is critical. Because it appears that many of America's public school teachers, who increasingly (if unintentionally) in recent years have left you in jeopardy in terms of the skills of their graduates, now are deliberately also leaving you vulnerable in terms of their ethics.

How much morality would you say is the right amount for America's public schools to try to instill in the students for whom they have responsibility? How much honesty? How much respect for life? How much compassion for the down and out?

No matter how little you expect on that score, your hopes may be too high. Published reports last week suggest that a majority of public school teachers think all such expectations are outside their job descriptions.

Wall Street Journal staff reporter Sonia L. Nazario wrote: "About 84 percent of public school parents want moral values taught in school, and 68 percent want educators to develop strict standards of 'right and wrong,' according to a Gallup Poll. . . . But polls also show that most teachers object to the concept of morality education on philosophical or practical grounds; many fear that such programs will stir up controversy in classrooms where diverse student bodies already cause plenty of headaches."

Indeed, Mark Beauvais, superintendent of the Concord, N.H., public school district, said bluntly, "It would be dangerous, sad, and boring to have one view of morality imposed on our people."

Writer Nazario noted: "After a decades-long drive for teachers to be value-neutral, some say they can't adjust to openly teaching right and wrong. *McGuffey Readers*, with their strong moral messages, have long been shunned for value-neutral texts and teacher-training courses. Texts describe the Pilgrims not as seekers of religious freedom but as 'people who take long trips.'"

So now, if you're a consumer of the typical products of American education, you face a double deficiency. The graduates you're expected to hire lack both the skills and the integrity you need to run your business. And what you find missing in your workplace is also increasingly missing in society at large.

Let's not be overly pious about the matter. Teaching our children to be scrupulously honest isn't the easiest thing in the world even when you can bring the full force of biblical precept to bear on the issue.

But what we're talking about here is a situation where most of the teachers involved say they want nothing to do with the subject. It's no longer an issue of trying and falling a little short. It's a case of ignoring the challenge from the beginning.

In fact, in the New Hampshire example, even the school board vowed to keep values education out of the classrooms. "This wipes out diversity and separation of church and state," said board vice president Barbara Kuhlman Brown. "It negates everything public schools stand for." And remember: Ms. Brown is no longer to be seen as an isolated radical. A majority of public school educators say they agree with her.

It's possible, if difficult, to imagine McDonald's and all its corporate counterparts engaging in a mammoth repair job for the damage inflicted by the failure of our schools to give their graduates the basic skills they need.

To ask them, however, to rebuild empty souls is something else again. The catch-22 is that the very teacher who desperately doesn't want to teach such things is absolutely the last one you want to require to teach them. Honesty and integrity that don't flow from deep within a person have little to do with the real thing.

Late-Inning Rally

BY JOEL BELZ
JANUARY 9, 1993

Imagine a spirited baseball game, if you will, going on for four decades now and ready to head into the last inning or two.

Playing offense is the "No Establishment of Religion" clause of the U.S. Constitution. Playing a discouraged defense is the "Free Exercise" clause of the same great document.

The game was meant to be played on a level field with an unbiased umpire. A few calls would probably go one way, and a few the other. That would mean, other things being equal, that the score would be close—which was exactly the design of those who wrote the rules.

But for as long as anyone can remember, the "No Establishment" team has been at bat, piling on run after run. When the "No Establishment" batters struck out, the umpires gave them more chances. Foul balls were called fair. Runners who were tagged out by a dozen feet were called safe.

But now, just as most "Free Exercise" fans have given up and headed home, a funny thing has happened. A few calls have started to go their way.

The officiating, mind you, is still nothing to crow about. Bizarre calls can be expected on just about any play.

But in Las Vegas, Nevada, last week, the "Free Exercise" team got a big hit. Eleven-year-old Kara Russell had been forbidden by her public school principal to sing "The First Noel" at a winter pageant because of the carol's Christian content. But then the Clark County school district reversed the principal's decision and said she could sing the song after all. The American Center for Law and Justice, a spinoff of Pat Robertson's Regent University in Virginia Beach, had threatened a lawsuit if Kara's freedom of speech and freedom of religion were not honored.

But did you notice that term "winter pageant"? Even though Kara got to sing, it wasn't at a Christmas program, mind you. Throughout the country, the very word *Christmas* is the kind of stuff from which the "No Establishment" team loves to manufacture runs. In Frederick County, Virginia, county school superintendent Thomas Malcolm actually issued a late October memo to all administrators requiring them to avoid using the word *Christmas* and to try talking instead about winter holidays, winter programs, and holiday parties. And, oh yes, said the memo, be careful about Easter as well; that is a spring holiday.

Thanks to a visit by Rutherford Institute attorney Melanie Davis, the superintendent's memo was temporarily rescinded and a runner from the "Free Exercise" team is at least on base. No run has been scored, however, because school officials think they have to give the matter "further study." Watch out for the umpire on this one.

In Austin, Texas, only a last-minute retraction and apology allowed the publication in the school newspaper of an essay by eighth-grader Christine Fisher. Christine's computer class was asked to write on "What Christmas Means to Me and Why." But when Christine included an inflammatory line claiming that "it is also the day that Christians celebrate Christ's birth," principal Joe Bartlett knew he had to rein her in. The essay could be published, he said, only if the line were changed to say, "It is also a day that people celebrate love." No, Christine's mother was told, that wasn't censorship but editorial license.

Not so, said Rutherford Institute's Kelly Shackelford. "Many school officials have terrible misconceptions about the law. Student-initiated religious expression is clearly protected by the U.S. Constitution."

Nor was that all. The feisty "Free Exercise" team is showing signs all over the field of coming out of a forty-year slump. For that, fans who like a good ball game should rejoice—at least a little bit.

But really, pleasing though these small victories might be, they need to be seen in context. The score is something like 272-3, with "Free Exercise" way behind. And the opposition has revised the rule book so thoroughly that the original is unrecognizable.

Think about it. What is there really to cheer about just because teachers can once more call Christmas Christmas—at least until the issue gets a little further study? If that is a reason to rejoice, please don't tell me any bad news.

Separating School and State

BY JOEL BELZ
FEBRUARY 25, 1995

When thoughtful people talk about the massive defects—or should I just call it the rottenness?—of the educational enterprise in America these days, they're usually referring to statist education. That's why two men who have been Secretary of Education in recent years (William Bennett and Lamar Alexander) are both calling now for the abolition of the whole Department of Education in Washington. Too bad we can't run every member of Congress through that same post for a few weeks so they would get just as realistic as the two former secretaries.

Not that private education on every level doesn't also have its own set of problems—economic, pedagogical, and even philosophical—that threaten its very existence.

But the huge mess we see all about us across the entire educational front exists in large measure because the state has been so profoundly involved in a task where it has no business. Even the stresses and strains felt in private education would be enormously alleviated if the government would just vacate the field.

That's why a new organization grabbed my attention a few days ago. Based in Fresno, California, it's called The Separation of School and State Alliance. The name plays off a most familiar theme but jars you with its application to a totally different relationship.

Nothing in the U.S. Constitution, of course, specifically advocates a total separation of church and state. Such a "wall" was alluded to once or twice by Thomas Jefferson, but it was actually erected in its present impermeable form only in recent years.

Yet if it's right to promote the separation of church and state because of the possibility of an inappropriate mutual influence of the two on each other, then it's even more important—if we're going to be consistent—to promote the total separation of school and state for exactly the same reasons. It should be just as distasteful (and alarming) to see state involvement in the local Jones Elementary School as it is for the state to serve as a sponsor of the local First Baptist Church.

Both churches and schools, if they are doing their jobs at all in the manner they ought to be doing them, are about ultimate ideas and values. That doesn't mean the tasks of churches and schools in God's scheme of things are identical. But both, if they are functioning properly, are so profoundly involved with shaping the minds, the hearts, and the souls of their people that it should be all but impossible for someone to draw a line saying where "education" leaves off and where "religion" picks up.

Least of all should an agency as clumsy as the government be charged with drawing such a delicate and nuanced line. If we have serious problems deciding whether the government is competent to be the carrier of mail or the scheduler of trains, why should we even be discussing whether that same government is competent to be discussing seriously with teenagers the purpose of history, the meaning of sexuality, or the significance of death?

Some will say, of course, that education doesn't need to talk about those subjects anyway and should leave them to parents and to churches. But such a cop-out fails to understand either what education is or the nature of questions young people naturally ask. Popular songs talk about all those subjects and much more—as well they should. To pretend that education can take place while ruling big chunks of life as "out of bounds" is to tell kids they can't hum or whistle certain tunes because those tunes might get them into certain religious or philosophical areas. Take the old lines from the musical, for example:

> *Love and marriage, love and marriage*
> *Go together like a horse and carriage. . . .*

Now ask yourself whether a public high school could stage that production these days without getting into heavy-duty "religious" discussions.

The goal, however, is not to sanitize education to the point that it's finally "religion-free" and therefore acceptable to everyone in a pluralistic society. The goal should be just the opposite. Great teachers are those who make every educational experience as robust and hearty and spicy and intimate and soul-searching as life itself is—and that, almost by definition, says the state shouldn't and can't be involved.

World magazine has no more basic assumption than this: All of life is religious. That's a preposterous claim for most modern American minds, who still think they can neatly divide life up into the scientific, the artistic, the emotional, the religious, etc. But instead of starting with ourselves and our own finite minds, we start with the assumption that God himself is the main reality. As Creator and the one who spoke all things into being, he is the central unifying force for all that is—or, as Paul says in Colossians, the one "by whom all things consist" (1:17, KJV). That, quite simply, is why all things are religious; everything in the universe revolves around the person of God.

Now, if that's your view of reality—and it should be for any serious person who takes the Bible at its word—any education that takes any other view of reality is going to be terribly inadequate and deficient. Note well: This obviously applies to any education that denies God as the center of all reality. But it applies just as certainly to any education that says you can pick any center of reality you want. For a biblical believer, that makes as much educational sense as a "pick any multiplication tables you want" approach makes for a good mathematician.

Long ago I heard about a traditional teacher who found herself in a progressive school where the principal said she could no longer teach the alphabet to kindergartners. Only when she protested did the principal finally give in a bit. "All right," he conceded, "but just make sure you don't teach the letters in alphabetical order!"

Is alphabetical order a "religious" idea? Well, is order itself a "religious" idea?

The answer is that every idea is profoundly religious. And if it's wrong for the state to sponsor two, three, or four hours of religion every week in church, then it's just that much more wrong for the state to sponsor twenty-five, thirty, or forty hours of religion every week in school.

More power to the folks in Fresno.

Idle Hands, Addled Brains

BY MARVIN OLASKY
AUGUST 26, 1995

When my four-year-old son threw an older brother's G.I. Joe on the asphalt and it broke into twenty pieces, Benjamin found that rage has consequences: He had to raise four dollars to replace it, which is harder than it may sound because his allowance is four cents a week.

Our family employment office did offer him job opportunities, however. First, Ben earned seventeen cents by picking up toys, at one cent apiece, and eighteen cents more by opening envelopes that had come in the day's mail, at one cent apiece.

Then, enjoying his prowess in money-making, he cleaned his room by stuffing into one corner what had been spread around the floor: a truck, two dinosaurs, seven library books, a wet bathing suit, and a dirty shirt. He wanted to know if that job was worth $500,000. I said that was a very big bit of money and that it wasn't a good idea to put a wet bathing suit on top of books. Ben was quick to move it. He was learning something about work.

Now that a new school year has begun, it's time to rethink our understanding of the role of labor in the lives of children. A hundred years ago many children worked too long, with sweatshops sometimes overshadowing schools. Now we've gone to the other extreme. Some children never do any work, and some teenagers are advised not to work during the school year either, out of concern that either their grades or social lives might suffer.

Such overconcern is folly. Studies highlight the long-term economic advantages of moderate employment during high school. Last year a study by Christopher Ruhm of the University of North Carolina-Greensboro examined earnings six to nine years after high school. Mr.

Ruhm found that high school seniors who had worked up to twenty hours a week were earning 22 percent more than classmates who did not work. He suggested that part-time jobs for seniors improve their knowledge of the job market and help them gain workplace skills. Another study, by Paul Barton of the Educational Testing Service, showed that moderate work did not hurt grades: High school students working twenty or fewer hours per week had better grades than either nonworkers or constant workers.

Other observers have noted that work leaves less time for mischief and mayhem. There is said to have been less sexual immorality in the Confederate Army during the Civil War than among the northern forces—perhaps because of different levels of biblical belief, perhaps because southern troops were more often on the march. Yankees in tents had camp-following prostitutes nearby; marching Southerners, traveling light, left ladies of the night behind and read pocket Bibles by candlelight. It is often better for teenagers today to spend time on the march than in the tents.

I'd suggest another benefit, from my own family's background. We've tried to give all our children some jobs from age four on, and we've seen that work experience can lead to a greater seriousness of purpose about schooling.

My oldest son, Pete, now eighteen, labored at a local supermarket on Saturdays during the past year and during the summer, alongside some former college students who didn't judge their talents accurately in relation to the job market. Pete persevered as a cashier, but the thought of doing that job for years is pushing him to serious study as he enters college rather than enrollment in one of the most popular courses at the University of Texas, "The History of Rock and Roll." (It runs neck and neck with "human sexuality.")

The lack of work experience among many who enter college is compounded when they do not pay any of their own way. Students not used to responsibility often flit from class to class; they learn that it is socially correct to have religious experiences at Woody Allen movies and not at fundamentalist services, but they do not prepare themselves to earn a living after graduation. Work as a supermarket cashier, on the other hand, requires adherence to a functional standard—"How many rings per minute do you average?"—not a set of trendy ideas.

When Ben hits the venerable age of five I will increase his allowance to something greater than four cents but less than $500,000; I think fifty cents each week is about right. But I will never want him to be in a situation where he feels no need to work.

Mid-Evil Education

BY MARVIN OLASKY
SEPTEMBER 21, 1996

"Don't know much about history" is the first line of a great song about love. As a new school year approaches, it's also an accurate description of the historical illiteracy that mediocre teaching and godless textbooks have aided and abetted.

Over the past twenty years some exasperated good teachers have taken to collecting examples of what their students write; an issue of the *Wilson Quarterly* published some, perhaps with a bit of Dr. Seuss thrown in. Here are some outstanding sentences concerning the Revolutionary Era: "The colonists won the war and no longer had to pay for taxis." "Delegates from the original thirteen states formed the Contented Congress." "Benjamin Franklin invented electricity by rubbing cats backwards. He also declared, 'A horse divided against itself cannot stand.'"

It gets worse, by the way, when students turn from American to world history. Then we learn that "The Ramons conquered the Geeks," and "Nero was a tyrant who tortured his subjects by playing the fiddle to them." We're also told that "William Tell shot an arrow through an apple while standing on his son's head," and that Sir Francis Drake, with the audacity typical of English sailors four centuries ago, "circumcised the world with a 100-foot clipper."

These comments may be funny, but research studies examining exactly what American citizens know are deeply troubling. One survey revealed that over half of high school seniors failed an easy multiple choice test about major events in American history; to pass, they only had to get 42 percent right! It's no wonder that many citizens cannot discern the emptiness of proposed governmental panaceas; they don't know that similar programs have been tried and have failed.

But not to worry: One thing students know (they have been taught to have high self-esteem) is that they are more knowledgeable than their ancestors. As one student wrote, "In midevil times most of the people were alliterate."

Since we now live in mid-evil times—we're on the information highway between Sodom and Gomorrah—historical illiteracy is only a symptom of deeper problems. After all, why study history if it, like life itself, is merely a tale of sound and fury, signifying nothing? If there is no God-given purpose to our existence, why not major in meaninglessness?

In an age of relativism, Christians need to keep stressing the basics—that if we are not here to glorify God and enjoy him forever, we might as well worship the false gods by eating and drinking and trying to be merry (although only a fool is merry in such circumstances). We need to keep insisting that there are only two choices, as Moses told the Israelites: Choose life and good, or death and evil.

But let's not overlook limited educational victories that can be won, even in the absence of deeper understandings. The trendy educational theorists of the past thirty years have demanded that history be taught in "relevant" ways, which means deemphasizing names and dates of major events and propagandizing about the capitalistic, homophobic, ethnocentric, patriarchal past that we are only now overcoming. Christians have to do a better job teaching both the details and the meaning.

We can do better by realizing that elementary school is the time (the Polly Parrot stage, as Dorothy Sayers called it) to fill children's heads with those facts of history. Kids love the darndest data, and if encouraged in that vein they will have all the base they need by the time they enter high school and are ready to argue.

We can do better by encouraging older students to debate the ideas that make history and to learn in the process that ideas have consequences. History, they will see, shows man's sin, man's occasional ability to learn from past errors, and man's opportunity, through God's grace, to sometimes get some things partially right. What could be more relevant to our current debates than to see when and how sweet-talkers, whether presidents or foreign dictators, showed that they should not be trusted?

We can do better by showing that efforts to do away with a societal emphasis on marriage, family, and private property are not new; they have been tried before, and they have failed before. (Students do pay attention to the effects of failure; one wrote, "Lincoln was shot by John Wilkes Booth. This ruined Booth's career.") The history of past government welfare failure, and past governmental attempts to minimize the role of religion, is certainly relevant.

But the deeper questions will still remain. Is Christ the Lord of history, or do the intellectual looters of the left have true wisdom? Does it matter if we don't know much about history? Does it matter if we don't know much about God?

Everything's OK at the Henhouse

BY JOEL BELZ
AUGUST 20, 1991

Contrary to everything you may have heard, there is no major problem with so-called "political correctness" on the nation's college and university campuses. It's just the figment of a few old worry-warts' imaginations.

And how do we know that the problem has been overblown so badly? We know it, and we can rest confident that the knowledge is certain, because of an "official" survey conducted in the last few weeks among "senior college administrators" on 359 campuses. They say overwhelmingly that no one should worry—that everything's OK.

The folks who took the survey are the same people who checked up with Reynard the fox and were told that everything was just fine at the henhouse. Earlier they had talked with the Nazis, who said not to worry about the Jews in Germany. They spoke also with Planned Parenthood, who calmed all fears about the fate of unborn babies in America.

Against all expectations, the researchers were able to provide remarkable reassurance. Simply put, alarms concerning possible intolerance by literal purists on America's campuses are totally unfounded.

The survey, according to the Knight-Ridder news service, focused on the 1990-91 school year, "when a spate of books and media accounts depicted U.S. higher education as being in a state of crisis over the political correctness issue." But never mind the spate of books, Knight-Ridder said. "The findings of the survey, the first of its kind, paint a very different picture."

The news service did acknowledge that "on many campuses, attempts to address intolerance have brought accusations from conservatives that schools have been pushing a liberal—or what has been described as a politically correct—point of view."

But according to our country's academic leaders, fewer than 10 percent of all colleges and universities have experienced actual controversy over such matters. Only 3 percent of the schools said they have experienced controversy over the political or cultural content of course texts. Only 4 percent reported any fusses over information presented in the classroom. And only 10 percent got exercised over invited speakers.

But instead of gullibly taking the campus officials' word for it, maybe we should explore whether things may actually be worse than anyone suggested—on at least two counts.

The first is that the "senior college administrators" on those 359 campuses have every reason, obviously, for denying that they have been allowing a kind of totalitarianism in their bailiwicks. What on earth should prompt Knight-Ridder's reporters to suppose that even a handful of chancellors and provosts would say, "Why, yes, of course, we regularly exhibit a certain kind of intolerance toward those who fail to hold to the accepted views of academia. In fact, we have frequent scuffles over such issues." That these folks would report even a 10 percent incidence of controversy suggests, on the face of it, that matters may really be much worse.

More to the point, however, are the lopsided statistics. Let's concede for the moment that the academic leaders are telling the truth when they say that only 3 percent of all the campuses surveyed had any controversy over the content of courses and curriculum. If that's actually the case, then America is saturated with campuses where lively debate has been snuffed out and where particular points of view so dominate that any opposition is barely suffered. In other words, the PC thought police have done their jobs so well that unruliness is no longer even threatened.

Almost certainly, both factors are at work. The report of the "senior college administrators" should by its very nature be significantly discounted. And then what's left of it should be feared because of what it still says.

Multicultural Opening Days

BY MARVIN OLASKY
APRIL 16, 1994

Reporters flocked to the parks on April 4 for major league baseball's opening day. This column is set nine days before, when I went back and forth between two other openings—one for the Pony League of northeast Austin, Texas, where I live, the other kicking off a series of workshops on multiculturalism and "diversity" at the University of Texas Department of Journalism, where I teach.

Our Pony League places 520 children (ages five through fourteen) on forty teams sponsored by local small businesses. Austin's leading advocates of multiculturalism tend to live in the affluent and overwhelmingly white western part of the city, but northeast Austin is racially and economically mixed. My sons' teammates are black, white, and brown, and many of the dads wear worn cowboy boots and drive old pickup trucks.

Opening day at the ballpark featured a color guard carrying the American flag, a local minister praying, and children of different sizes and skin colors taking off their caps and putting hands over hearts as "The National Anthem" was sung. Opening day at the journalism department featured a professor's confession that he had not fully come to grips with America's history of "genocide and slavery."

The workshop, which was "mandatory" for faculty members, began with a university official reporting the results of a student survey: Minority students were said to complain about sometimes "being ignored" and other times receiving "glances." Then the question was thrown at a panel of black and Hispanic juniors and seniors: "Have you experienced discrimination?" Several professorial faces fell when the students sounded as if they had grown up playing baseball: "I haven't experienced any directly. . . . Hard work pays off. . . . If you take the initiative you can make things happen. . . . Sometimes I think we spend too much time complaining."

The workshop got back on track when several role-model professors from other departments explained the real agenda. "Teaching is a form of radical politics," one said, "my way of helping to reshape the world." Another structures his course to push students slowly to the left: " I want 100 percent converts, I really do." He is proud of his successes: "Sometimes the most conservative students become the most rabid."

Some older journalism professors who grew up with ideas of press objectivity seemed uneasy about deliberate attempts to radicalize students, but a younger professor replied, "It's our responsibility to make them think that way. So there." There was nervous laughter, but the path to university success is clear.

The last hour of the workshop featured more discussion about subtle ways to politicize courses, perhaps by avoiding hard facts and instead emphasizing feelings of oppression. The merging of personal and ideological agendas became obvious here; one male professor complained, "I've had experiences wanting to talk about feelings with men who I thought were friends, and they want to talk about baseball scores."

That was certainly my feeling after four hours of reeducation, so I hurried back to northeast Austin. On one field, a black pitcher was striking out batters and winning cheers from teammates and parents, regardless of race. On another field, a white batter hit a home run and received similar hurrahs. *E pluribus unum*: The culture of baseball dominates. My wife and I have gone to countless games since 1986, and neither of us nor any of our children ever remembers hearing an angry racial epithet.

The difference between baseball and academic culture is not only that the latter is dominated by the political left. Baseball emphasizes competition and measurement of performance; academia is increasingly touchy-feely. The University of Texas, like baseball, was segregated during the first half of the century, but American universities have not followed baseball in correcting that wrong by applying the same set of objective criteria (batting averages or test results) to everyone; the UT Law School is now being sued for favoring black and Hispanic applicants for admission.

"Scores, scores, scores, too much emphasis on scores," one organizer of the workshop erupted when she was asked why some white males are unhappy with university policies. But competition broke down baseball's color line without producing a sense of unfairness. Scorecards (like bottom lines) are discrimination's enemies. If universities stress good feelings over good grades, they will produce only the Balkans.

Opening day for the multicultural workshops ended with an air of self-congratulation. "I'm feeling right down to my toes the need for diversity," said an assistant professor hoping for tenure. Opening day at the Pony League ended with the coach of one sloppy, losing team telling his charges, "The next practice will be real tough, and we'll have extra laps."

The Prime Concern: Invaders Within

BY MARVIN OLASKY
OCTOBER 8, 1994

Catch me before I chuckle again: Whenever someone says immigration from Mexico will destroy Texas, I can't help laughing. What I saw during my September 23-25 weekend in Austin, Texas, and Juarez, Mexico, reminded me that tenured barbarians are already ravaging our republic, and that we should rein in those rascals and not worry so much about immigrants who value work and family.

The weekend festivities began at a time in the Republic when thoughts usually turn to football games. At 4 P.M. on Friday my colleagues in The University of Texas at Austin journalism department voted for a policy statement on "diversity" that commits the department to "increasing opportunities" for homosexual professors and students and gives such folks a legal handle if they decide to sue. This in a Texas where sodomy is still a crime.

I've learned in the journalism department not to waste my breath on appeals to morality, but I thought a basic level of prudence was still present. Although the UT administration has put condom machines in dormitories, it still does not want professors to be so obviously thumbing their noses at our generally conservative, long-suffering taxpayers. When I reminded my colleagues that they were going beyond university policy and stroking folks who often act contrary to Texas law, one (who receives a UT salary of over $50,000) said, "We'll secede from the university, [profanity]," and another (who is openly homosexual) said, "I try to violate university policy at least once a day."

Some of my colleagues train future reporters and editors to sneer whenever they hear Texas conservatives use the f-word, *family*. Others do not engage in deliberate destruction but have unthinkingly absorbed the values of liberal academic culture and are passing them on. In either case, journalism students—the future media gatekeepers—are in bad hands.

I spent the next day in a setting far different from that of our air-conditioned conference room. Since a cold front had come in, the temperature was only about 90 in the shadeless newer *colonia* on the outskirts of Juarez, where thousands of migrants from the interior of Mexico live in cardboard shacks on plots of barren dirt that they have bought. Many have come to work for about $2,000 a year in Juarez factories.

UT Marxists seeing this would immediately yell, "Capitalist exploitation." But Presbyterian minister Moises Zapata then showed me around another poor community, one that has been around a bit longer. There cardboard has given way to cement block and ornamental grillwork, and houses have fans. At a fifteen-year-old settlement farther down the road, there are handsome houses, small trees, paved roads, some air conditioners, and even a satellite dish. "Some of the *colonia* here are like slums in the States," one missionary pointed out, "but there the poor stay poor because of welfare dependency. Here you can see progress: People have to work."

An emphasis on hard work and family underlies the transformation, but once a basic level of comfort is achieved, stagnation sometimes sets in. That's why another minister, Josue Mayo, led a family values Sunday school class at the middle-class Eglesia Renovacion in Juarez on September 25, basing his teaching on Ephesians 5:22-25: "Wives, submit to your husbands as to the Lord. . . . Husbands, love your wives, just as Christ loved the church and gave himself up for her." Pastor Mayo noted—here's a rough translation—"We honor God by obeying him, and when we obey him we have family and economic progress."

God's rules also point the way to progress north of the border. The truly New Texas is and should be multicultural ethnically and racially, but it needs common values concerning the importance of family and work; a culture with firm foundations cannot be built on the sand of radical individual autonomy. Immigrants who have lived out these common values should be welcome. That's why, under the Olasky immigration policy, men who have been married for at least ten years and have worked steadily during that period would be accepted for immigration, along with their wives and children. (Noncitizens would not be eligible for governmental welfare, however.)

The real threat to Texas resides in university departments such as my own. The University of Texas at Austin, like many other schools, has etched on its administration building the words of John 8:32, "You shall know the truth, and the truth shall make you free." Alas, the opposite tendency is also operative: lies heard in the classroom enslave millions.

Will immigration destroy Texas values? The work and family ethic is already on life support, holding on only through new infusions of a biblical worldview. As Moises Zapata puts it, "Make a pagan rich and you worsen his condition, because instead of getting drunk only once a week on weekends, he can now afford to drink steadily and purchase pornography and prostitutes." Juarez and Austin both have that problem. "Educate a pagan and you worsen *your* condition," Zapata says, "because you now have a smart enemy." That's the prime problem at most Texan universities. "The only solution is Jesus Christ," Zapata concludes.

Economics

Deferring Our Desires

BY JOEL BELZ
MAY 11, 1987

Economists Frank Levy and Richard Michel have calculated [that] in 1949 it took just 14 percent of an average 30-year-old man's paycheck to make the payments on an average home. By 1985 the figure was 44 percent."

That's the kind of comparison that grabs your attention and in the process makes you feel a little sorry for yourself, or at least for your children if you were blessed to get your own mortgage before 1977 or so.

Instead of feeling a little sorry, maybe we should feel a little guilty.

Robert Kuttner's point in quoting Levy and Michel in last week's *New Republic* was to suggest that a family home is fast becoming a luxury available only to the wealthy—or to those who inherited enough money from their parents to buy a house for themselves.

I believe Kuttner, while making an intriguing point, misses a more important one. The point he misses is that while the relative cost of housing may indeed have increased dramatically since 1949, something else has increased even more dramatically—our expectations of what life owes us.

Try to think of a single person in your whole acquaintance who lives in a home less comfortable than the one his or her parents had at the same stage in life. Most of us, clearly, arrived at young adulthood assuming some kind of inalienable right to three bedrooms, two baths, a garbage disposal, and at least one fireplace. No, that's not a caricature—it is literally what peer pressure has led us to expect of life.

My point here has little to do with the price of houses either now or forty years ago. It has instead to do with our society's inability to defer the gratification of its desires. The main reason average housing takes 44 percent out of a person's paycheck now as opposed to 14 percent a generation ago is that the average person's expectations for the housing he absolutely must have are so much greater than they used to be. The same thing is true for cars, clothes, leisure time, travel, and all the other things that drive our family budgets up, up, and up.

We Christians are, in this regard, virtually indistinguishable from the society we live in. And by blending in with our surroundings, we have missed a strategic opportunity for witness to a key element of the Gospel.

Make no mistake here. This is not another call to simple living, at least not on a permanent basis. The guilt I suggest we ought to feel has less to do with enjoying the good things God has made than it does with when we are privileged to enjoy them. Like the world around us, we Christians tend to assume that early enjoyment is our prerogative.

But Christians, of all people, should understand that the MasterCard mentality is not the way to master life. The pattern Jesus established was one of deferring desires—not because the fulfillment of desires is wrong, but because "my time has not yet come." Most of us think our time has come five minutes after the desire first pops into our minds.

Yet few concepts are more central to a Christian way of thinking than the idea of deferring a present desire—in the confidence that something richer lies down the road. It is a constant and unrelenting theme of Scripture.

"Unless a kernel of wheat falls into the ground and dies," Jesus said in effect, "it cannot bear fruit" (John 12:24). Deferral now, rich reward later. He understood the concept perfectly, and his obedience to the point of death on the cross is, of course, the key to his and our future glory.

The theme permeates our lives. Train now, win the game later. Pull the weeds now, enjoy the sweet corn later. Skip the dessert now, enjoy a trim waistline later.

The principle is everywhere except in our consumer consciousness. There, the infection still rages. And for such an infection to rage within the Christian community is costly in two ways.

First, it is costly in terms of wasted resources. In following the world's pattern of satisfying so many of our desires almost as soon as we feel them, we are spending far more than we should on interest and carrying charges. We would literally have 50 percent more to spend on what we want—maybe even 100 percent more—if we patiently waited until the resources were in hand instead of buying right now. Think what impact that could have on the underfinanced ministries of God's kingdom.

Second, it is costly in terms of a wasted witness. If Christians were known around the world as people who through their patience, thrift, and keen sense of priorities lived prosperous lives, the Gospel they preach and teach would have more credibility than it does now when so many of us spend most of our years playing catch-up with the finance companies.

Mr. Kuttner, the problem isn't that too few of us have inherited money from our parents to buy houses of the style in which we have become accustomed to live. The problem is our impatience with living in a slightly lesser style. It would be a great thing if Christians could teach such a lesson to the world. But before we can teach it persuasively, we'll probably have to learn it for ourselves.

Being Half Right Doesn't Work

BY JOEL BELZ
NOVEMBER 28, 1992

Two practical reasons should prompt us to keep the simple motto "In God we trust" on our currency and our coins.

The first is that it's such an ever-present reminder. You can't get through a typical day without reaching into your pocket or wallet for some cash—and right there, several times every day, is a memory jogger about your ultimate allegiance.

The second reason is that it's precisely while you're using cash—something you're very much tempted to put your trust in—that you need to be taught again that your trust actually belongs somewhere else.

We do tend, you know, to trust in money. That's true even of us Christians—as was demonstrated in the recent elections. A few evangelicals voted as if ideological issues were paramount. But just as many seemed to be saying that economic issues matter most. As evangelical theologian Norman Geisler put it in a *World* interview last week, even evangelicals tended in large numbers to vote "money ahead of morals, power ahead of principles."

Or, to put it more crassly, even evangelicals tended to express their trust more in the dollar bill itself than they did in the God addressed by the motto on the dollar bill.

The big irony, of course, is that just as ideological Marxism has taken a monstrous tumble around the world, voters in the United States of America have given credence to a basic tenet of Marxism—that human beings are guided ultimately by material issues. They may say they're concerned about deficit spending and family values or other lofty ideals, but such expressions are really just so much hokum when people go into the voting booth during even slightly hard financial times. Bill Clinton was mirroring Marx when he and his campaign advisers assumed that people ultimately vote their pocketbooks; Americans proved them right.

So the U.S. finds itself now in the awkward situation of having won the ideological war internationally but still feeling—and even looking—like a loser. How can that be?

It happens because God's laws are established in such a manner that you can't play games with him. He doesn't let you acknowledge that he's right part of the time and then exclude him from the rest of your thinking. Yet that's just what our society has tried, and keeps on trying, to do.

America discovered early on that a certain economic approach—commonly referred to as the free market—worked wonderfully. For several centuries it produced a combination of personal freedom and material bounty unmatched in human history. And a high proportion of America's population enjoyed that freedom and bounty; even those who didn't share in such blessings at least sensed they had a chance to.

But make no mistake; this was no raw, unqualified free enterprise at work. It was a much more complex package than that. Almost always, there was a hefty confidence that God was doing something here in a New World that he hadn't done for a while. Many folks thought God was giving "his people" a chance again to do what Israel had tried, but failed, to do: to work hard, exercise vigorous industry, and honor God in the process. Here in America, that effort was often sullied—sometimes with terrible injustice, sometimes with greed, almost always with varying degrees of misunderstanding and error. But the "In God we trust" motto was also more than a shibboleth.

Yet just like Israel, the U.S. edged through the years more and more toward self-reliance and away from God-reliance. America even made a fetish of that rebellion. Year by year we found new ways to tell God where he was permitted to be part of public society and where he would not be welcome. And we assumed all the while that we could make his splendidly designed economic plans work to our hearts' content, even while shutting him out of the rest of our lives.

God is not mocked. There he is—right on the bills and the coins we so much want to work for us, reminding us almost every hour of every day of our faithlessness. How much closer does the reminder need to be?

Our Own Worst Enemies

BY JOEL BELZ
DECEMBER 12, 1992

One of the quickest ways to kill a good idea is to overstate it.

It's with that in mind that I think many conservatives become their own worst enemies when they accuse the federal government of theft. For many years I've heard the argument that when Uncle Sam taxes us and then passes on the proceeds of our taxes to someone else, he is acting just like a burglar in a holdup. Because the government has the power to put us in jail if we don't pay up, the argument goes, and since the money is taken without our assent and then put in someone else's pocket, the result is nothing short of thievery.

Such language is strong and colorful, but it doesn't fit logic or the Bible.

Logically, the power to tax is the power to make one person rich and the next person poor. The essence of taxation is the clout to redistribute wealth. It has always been so—and to suggest that some taxation resorts to such an evil while other taxation is pristine and innocent of the crime is naive.

Even those with the narrowest view of government agree, for example, that providing for a nation's military defense is an appropriate role for government. But even that activity takes money from your pocket and mine and puts it in the hands of newly recruited privates in the army, their commanding generals, and the clothing manufacturers who make uniforms for both of them. And if you argue that such redistribution of wealth is only an incidental result of the decision to establish a military force, you haven't been watching carefully for the last twenty years when so many futile efforts have been waged to close down particular military bases. It is precisely because wealth is being redistributed that the bases are preserved; it has nothing whatsoever to do with military strategy.

So, of all those dollars being directed toward "the military," which have been collected through a government's legitimate right to tax? And which are merely "legalized theft"? It's not all that easy to sort out such dollars—and maybe not even right to do so if it were easy.

Another example: A few libertarian purists still deny the government should be involved in building roads and highways. But most of us concede that as a legitimate role. Yet it is impossible to engage in that activity without producing profound redistribution of wealth; indeed, such redistribution is often one of the declared goals of road-building, as when a modern highway is planned for the very purpose of stimulating the economy of a particular region.

Further, as pointed out a generation ago by the late black leader Whitney Young, urban expressways have from their beginning been a means of subsidizing suburban housing. The same people who complain about federally funded welfare housing have no scruples about riding on federally funded highways to reach their homes in the suburbs—which, incidentally, are also subsidized with generous income tax deductions for mortgage interest.

The point here is not to defend the wisdom or prudence of such subsidies and such redistribution of wealth; very often they are unwise and imprudent.

The point instead is simply to remind ourselves that implicit in the power of the state to tax is the power also to recirculate wealth. The making of public policy always brings with it the power to exercise the judgment that some citizens can afford to pay to accomplish costly goals for other citizens.

The Bible reminds us that sometimes this will be done with wisdom and sometimes it will be done with foolishness and even harshness. But the Bible nowhere suggests that it is not the prerogative of the state to do it. Instead of outlining what government may tax for and what it may not tax for, Paul urges Timothy to pray for leaders whose policy-making will lead to "peaceful and quiet lives" for citizens who want to pursue godliness and holiness (1 Timothy 2:2).

Our arguments about taxation (and especially about federal taxation) would be stronger if we focused on the issues of wisdom and foolishness instead of on the right of the government to do what it does. The right has been ordained by God. How that right is carried out is the issue—just as it is with every other privilege God gives us.

Free Market Law-Busters

BY JOEL BELZ
MARCH 18, 1995

In economics, as anywhere, breaking God's law has a price.

Breaking God's law is always a risky thing to do. But breaking some of his laws appears riskier than breaking others. Or at the very least, the potential damage becomes obvious a lot sooner when you break some laws than when you break others.

Try breaking God's law of gravity, for example, and you'll discover with alarming immediacy the seriousness of your error. Break his laws of sexuality, and it may take a while longer to discover the penalty for your disobedience. But either way make no mistake—God's laws simply can't be broken. If you don't pay now, you'll pay later.

Although folks everywhere resist the idea, God has similar systems of laws at work in every realm of life. Sometimes those laws are easily discernible (as in the case of gravity), and we catch on fairly quickly. Sometimes the laws seem more obscure, and it takes us forever to get God's message.

In the realm of economics, human society has been making some startling rediscoveries in the last few years about how God's laws work. In simplest terms, people have been learning again the potent force of free markets. To the extent that such discoveries keep unfolding and people everywhere respond obediently to God's pattern for things, rich productivity and human freedom seem likely.

But it's not, apparently, an easy lesson to catch on to. Throughout the world the dark warning keeps going out that such a system just can't be trusted—that however appealing it may be right now after the fall of communism and the demise of still more Socialist societies, free exchange is still suspect.

Just last week, U.S. Rep. Charles Schumer (D-N.Y.) complained in a press conference about the high cost of breakfast cereals, saying that in that arena "the free market has quit working. We're paying caviar prices for corn flake flavor."

At a five-day conference last week in Agra, India, I was reminded that evangelical Christians too can be deeply suspicious of the so-called "free market." The development of that market in the last few years—and especially the impact of that development on the poor people of the world— was the focus of attention for 120 of us who gathered from forty-two nations around the world.

For many of those people, to equate free market principles with the law of God is close to blasphemy. So I want to be careful in my assertion.

But I think it is even more demeaning to the character of God to say what many Christians blithely claim—that any one system of economics is the same in God's eyes as any other system. To claim, as biblical Christians do, that God knows everything but has no evaluative opinion about what he knows, is the ultimate putdown. Does God, the Creator of the heavens and the earth, have opinions about what is beautiful? Is the one who created the musical scales and the chirps of the birds tone-deaf when it comes to deciding whether some music is good and other music is bad?

If such people mean to say that Christians should be prepared to live under any kind of economic system, just as they should under any political system, I agree. But that's a different argument.

Recognition of God's creation ordinances, mind you, never means slavery to them. Real obedience always means glorious freedom.

Where is that more evident than in the flight of an airliner? As our Delta L-1011 lifted off from the Delhi airport to head back toward Frankfurt, Germany, I couldn't help musing, What if the Lockheed engineers (and the Wright brothers before them) had simply frozen themselves in a permanent sulk over the laws of gravity? But instead, they gave those laws their great respect, cooperated fully with them, and made a 200-ton airplane fly.

This free market theory that I think God has established as a basic building block of human society is pretty elementary. It refers to two parties making a voluntary and lawful agreement to exchange items of value.

When they do so, God has planned things so that both parties can walk away from that exchange happier than they were when they approached it, and both of them actually have the opportunity also to be wealthier. It makes as much sense as a plane flying—but it works! It works everywhere, in every culture, in every era of history. It works not because Adam Smith said it would, but because God planned that it would.

Can the simple scenario be abused? Of course it can be—and regularly is. But the abuse of anything is no signal that the thing itself is wrong, or even that it's suspicious. Take sex, for example. The whole mystery in which our sexuality is packaged is a textbook case of God's having designed something to perfection only to have us muck it up with a zillion kinds of abuse. Yet the foulest of our abuses takes nothing from the glory of God's original design.

The same is true with the market economy. Its beauty can be obscured with greed, with laziness, with impatience, with pride, and with failure to love our neighbor as ourselves. But none of those sins takes away from the magnificence of the original model.

All of which is not to say that the GHP (that's the gross heavenly product) in God's eternal kingdom will be measured in U.S. dollars. One of the problems friends of the market economy always face is that they're asked to defend historic American abuses of the free market system. What's partly odd about that is that the United States isn't really a very pure example at all of a market economy at work. Thousands of restraints have been tacked on, and any resemblance between a classic market economy and what you see today in America is almost coincidental.

A Christian's responsibility is to learn to distinguish between the obedient use of God's systems on the one hand and the disobedient abuse on the other. Putting a railing around a 100-foot-high landing is an obedient response to God's law of gravity; jumping off that landing is a disobedient abuse. Similar responses need to be spelled out for virtually all God's marvelous systems—including his economic systems. And it's not always easy to decide who puts up all the various railings. Will it be individuals and voluntary groups, or will it be the state, backed by force?

But don't let those questions make you back off from the glory of one of God's great gifts. From the beginning of time, it's been his design to let two people swap things of value on a free and legal basis and both profit from the experience. When something goes wrong in that process, it's our fault—not his.

Race

One at a Time

BY JOEL BELZ
NOVEMBER 5, 1993

I've heard for as long as I can remember that men of German descent tend to be cold, insensitive, and unfeeling toward their wives. Since I'm of German ancestry, the charge might occasionally have tended to bother me a bit—except, of course, that I'm cold, insensitive, unfeeling, and unaffected by ethnic slurs.

I've also heard that people whose grandparents were Italian (or was it Irish?) tend to have uncontrollably fiery tempers. Since a fellow with an Italian name just married one of my daughters, the report has potential for giving me some concern.

And since British people have a reputation for bland and uninteresting food, I might tend to skip dinner invitations from folks with pointedly Anglo-Saxon names.

But the fact is that I've tended largely to ignore all three of these insults to various people—and not merely because I know them to be false, which I don't. Indeed, my guess is that they are all actually based on some strong statistical elements of truth.

All this comes to mind because of the wide-open controversy now raging in both academic and journalistic circles over the new book *The Bell Curve* by Charles Murray and the late Richard Herrnstein. *The Bell Curve* purports to demonstrate statistically that there are IQ differences between blacks and whites in the United States, significantly to the detriment of blacks. It is, of course, explosive stuff.

There's apparently not much real debate over whether *The Bell*

Curve's data are right. As Tom Morgenthau reports in *Newsweek*, the assertion that blacks score significantly lower than whites on IQ tests and other measures of cognitive ability "is nothing new . . . educators and psychologists have known for years that the difference between the mean (or average) white IQ and the mean black IQ is 15 points—a score of 100 compared with a score of 85."

Mr. Morgenthau didn't complicate his report by also noting that there's little disagreement that Caucasian Americans are inferior to Orientals on some of the same tests.

But as soon as academics and commentators start trying to figure out what all this means, the fur starts flying. This happens partly because so many folks can't agree on why the statistics come out as they do (raising all sorts of questions about racism), and partly because so many other folks can't agree on what we ought to do as a result (raising all sorts of questions about public policy).

In the midst of such confusion, Christians should say loudly and clearly, "Forget it! It doesn't matter! It doesn't matter for two important reasons."

First, all this doesn't matter because every group of humans everywhere is messed up somehow. Just suppose for a moment that the worst thing you could say about any race or ethnic group were true. What will always come back to haunt you is that the worst thing somebody else says about your own race is also probably true—at least in some measure. The best proof of that is that virtually every one of us has inferiority feelings of some sort—and if we don't, we should. People who don't feel inferior about something are usually pretty obnoxious folks.

Theologically, this is so because we are fallen people—all of us. That fall is so profound that in one sense the term refers to our actual condition, and in another sense even to our mistaken perception of that condition. We are that thoroughly messed up.

We're all in this together. Who can look with disdain on any other group? If this week's statistics reveal one group's deficiency, we need wait only until next month's numbers to have our own shortcomings blazed forth.

I'm not sure whether the average black is 15 points behind the average white on standardized IQ tests, but even if it were proved to me that such is the case, I'd still be forced to say that it doesn't matter. For all I know, even with a 15 point edge, whites are nowhere nearly smart enough to put together an accurate IQ test.

But second, such group tendencies really mean very little in the big scope of things. The great stories in human history have always had less to do with the foibles and failures (or even the successes) of whole groups than with individuals rising above the group and all its problems.

And while God has never ignored groups in his grand scheme of things, and indeed is ultimately concerned with assembling the most incredible group of people imaginable to live with him for all eternity, he does that through a remarkable means. God is building his new group through a subtractive process of taking individuals away, one at a time, from all existing groups to which we get so attached and of which we get too proud.

He took Abram and separated him from his family in Ur and told him he'd become a father figure in a new group. He split Daniel and Esther off from their familiar settings and used them both in unlikely, unfamiliar, and very diverse contexts to work out brand-new ideas. He did the same with the fellow who then became known as the apostle Paul. In more recent years he's yanked people like John Newton, William Carey, and Charles Colson away from their diverse affinity groups to transplant them into his own royal family. It's a slow process, doing all this one by one—but that's how God generally deals with people.

What God does so painstakingly, human beings ought not to try to do more grandly. If God brings correction and progress to his people one person at a time, why do we get so intent on doing it whole ethnic groups, whole races, or whole nations at a time?

That is one of the things many of us find so objectionable about big and overwhelming statist solutions to problems like IQ scores deemed to be a little low or health care availability judged to be unevenly available or gross national product considered to be unjustly distributed.

For anyone to assume an ability to conceive detailed overall solutions to all that brokenness is to be as arrogant as it would be for any human, upon spying a splattered egg, to propose repackaging it neatly in its shell. Some brokenness, we need to learn to admit, is so profound that the original whole simply can't be reassembled.

That's not an ultimately pessimistic view. It's pessimistic only about one solution that has failed repeatedly.

God's solution, meanwhile, works very well. The way to fix society's hurts, bruises, and broken pieces is to address them the same way he does—one person at a time. It might surprise us how fast a new and much healthier group begins to reappear.

When Fault Lines Coincide

BY JOEL BELZ
NOVEMBER 4, 1995

With all the talk of racial polarization since the mid-October "Million Man March" in Washington, it's easy to lose sight of an even more profound chasm Louis Farrakhan's big event may have begun to split wide open. The huge chasm yawns between historic Christianity on the one hand and black Islam on the other.

Not that the racial divide should be minimized. As Fred Barnes of *The Weekly Standard* said on *The McLaughlin Group*, "Louis Farrakhan, with his march, put himself squarely into the middle of the 1996 election." And he did it not at all by being a reconciler, but by building bluntly on his ugly style of driving wedges between groups of people.

Coming hard on the heels of the O.J. Simpson verdict, the Farrakhan march struck a strange exclamation point at the end of a depressing paragraph—a paragraph that had explained all too clearly how little the last generation of Americans has really gained in terms of racial harmony. Blacks and whites may actually be farther, and more significantly, apart than we've ever been before.

All of which makes the issues of religion and faith that much more critical. So long as the fault line separating Christians and Muslims runs in a different direction from the one traditionally dividing blacks and whites, the gnarled grains tend to prevent a split right down the middle. But when the fault lines begin to coincide, an eerie prospect looms.

It is not, after all, just any old division. It is instead the biblical archetype of cleavages—the split that happened in Genesis and has continued to divide the human family ever since. Everyone since Abraham (actually, everyone since Adam) has either been numbered in Abraham's legitimate family or seen—even by God—as an outsider. It's impossible to imagine a more profound division.

Yet it's important to add quickly that, from a biblical perspective, this division has absolutely nothing to do with race. Even if the story starts with the account of Ishmael and Isaac, who were respectively Abraham's illegitimate and legitimate sons, it doesn't take much Bible reading to discover that race is not what ultimately matters to God.

Opportunists—including Mr. Farrakhan—will regularly try to suggest that the issues are primarily racial, or national, or regional, or having to do with economic class. There will be huge debates, as there were in Congress last week, about whether the U.S. embassy to Israel should be in Tel Aviv, where it's been since 1948, or in Jerusalem, where Jews want it and the Islamic people don't. There will continue to be bitter differences over sites in Jerusalem—known as a holy city to Jewish, Muslim, and even some Christian people.

But those issues are not the great divide God is concerned with.

Louis Farrakhan refers repeatedly to the great divide that God sees— but he regularly comes down on the wrong side.

Again and again Mr. Farrakhan brings up the subject of atonement. Like all of us, Mr. Farrakhan is also tempted first to think that through hard work, self-discipline, and proper regimentation, we might be able to set straight what has gone wrong. Indeed, there's a certain appeal to the message of his Black Muslims, coming after more than a generation of failed governmental efforts. Here is self-help, self-reliance—or, in Mr. Farrakhan's words, self-atonement.

That, sadly, is what makes the Farrakhan message both doubly and desperately wrong. To the enormous injury of deepening the racial divide, he adds the eternal hurt of preaching a message of altogether false hope.

For the message of the Bible, and the burden of the Christian Gospel, is that we cannot in the end pull ourselves up by our own bootstraps. No matter how neat our suits and bow ties may make us look compared to the slovenly dress of those about us, we have still dressed up only the external man. No matter how much we talk about discipline and being a real man and taking duty seriously—all of which are admirably present in the Farrakhan gospel—it will still come to nothing if the real goal is to measure up to God's standard.

None of Abraham's children—the Muslim children of Ishmael, the Jewish children of Isaac, or even the Christian children who trace their roots back to this remarkable father of many—can ultimately afford such a message of works. None of us can afford it because none of us can perform it. What we all need instead is a message of grace, of atonement by someone outside our own experience.

Most American blacks once reveled in such a Gospel. Many still do.

But in offering so many of them something less right now, Louis Farrakhan is betraying rather than helping the people of his own race. But the fact that the betrayal is so attractive makes it all the more dangerous.

Why Affirmative Action Is Harmful

BY MARVIN OLASKY
APRIL 13, 1996

A California referendum, a Texas case, congressional legislation—affirmative action is being debated among God's children throughout the land once again, with learned discourses on both sides. I'm not a very good "briefer," as they say in Washington, because I tend to throw complications at politicians who want simple answers, but on this issue I can keep it simple.

Here goes: God is our Father. I'm a father too. And although I can in no way fathom the depths of God's mind, I can know what God thinks about race from reading the Bible. I can get a sense of his emphasis on the importance of evenhanded treatment for all his children from the way my children—created in God's image—explode when they believe they have been treated unfairly.

First, what God thinks about racial and ethnic barriers: The New Testament very clearly and repeatedly says that we are to concern ourselves with "sin, not skin," as Glenn Loury puts it. What's not in the Bible speaks almost as loudly as what is: In sixty-six books of the Old and New Testaments, filled with descriptions of historical figures from three continents, flesh color is left out of the IDs. In the Bible, man's surface is no big deal.

Second, my experience as a father of four sons (three pink, one brown) also suggests that we just say no to differential treatment. Were all my children's first words, "It's not fair"? Maybe not, but any show of favoritism, real or supposed, is a sure cause of trouble, as it should be. I am charged to teach my children about God by showing evenhandedness—and I also teach them about our need for Christ when I mess up.

For those who want detailed analysis of the wrongness in practice of government racial preferences, I'd suggest reading Terry Eastland's excellent new book *Ending Affirmative Action*. But I, facing the constraints of a column, can keep it simple: Two wrongs don't make a right. Restitution is an important biblical concept, and maybe restitution for slavery would have worked after the Civil War, with help going directly to injured parties, although the complexities even then would have made the task daunting.

Today, however, we have the spectacle of job and educational prospects taken from the descendants of Irish, Italian, and other immigrants, who themselves faced great discrimination, and given to minority members and all women, whether or not their ancestors were enslaved. This affirmative action has no biblical base.

The last generation's leading liberal Supreme Court justice, William O. Douglas, argued that "Racial discrimination against a white is as unconstitutional as race discrimination against a black." Justice Thurgood Marshall responded to that statement by telling Mr. Douglas, "You guys have been practicing discrimination for years. Now it's our turn." That response is natural and understandable, but it is tragic for a simple reason: Two wrongs don't make a right.

The current emphasis on race leads us to overlook the wisdom T.S. Eliot once offered: "Do we want a wool sweater? We need to plant the grass to feed the sheep to get the wool to make a sweater." If we want twenty-first-century America (unless Christ comes first) not to be a country divided into white, black, brown, yellow, and red factions at war with each other, then we had better plant the right sort of grass now, instead of sitting back as weeds sprout. If we hope to move toward a biblical lack of race-consciousness, we are not well served by measures that make race the prime defining characteristic, trumping faith and character.

We can't make a big deal out of race in so many areas of our lives without making it a big deal in our minds—and it doesn't have to be that way. Making skin more important than sin is one of the sins that God can empower us to overcome. The epistle-writing Paul would not have instructed the Galatians and the Colossians that in Christ "there is neither Jew nor Greek" if it were impossible for our minds to be freed from racial and ethnic obsession.

God is the father of children of different races. I'm a father like that too. God tells us to pay attention to sin, not skin, and I believe him. I look to the future and ask, Do I want my family divided against itself by government-mandated unfairness, no matter whom it benefits? No. And if I don't want that in my own family, why would I want it in my country?

Popular Culture

Sinless Gump

BY MARVIN OLASKY
AUGUST 13, 1994

Never say that Hollywood does not respond to pressure from Christians protesting promiscuous sex, violence, and obscenity in the movies. This summer's surprise box-office sensation, *Forrest Gump*, has none of these. Gump is a saint who honors his mother, consistently loves one girl/woman, and never gets angry. Some evangelicals have called him a role model. *Movieguide*, a Christian publication "dedicated to redeeming the values of the media according to biblical principles," gave the film four stars and commended Gump's "purity of vision."

There's one main problem with such praise: That purity of vision does not include Christ. It doesn't need to because, according to Wendy Finerman, co-producer of the movie, "the child-like innocence of Forrest Gump is what we all once had" and need to develop anew. Gump's virtues are a byproduct of his IQ of 75: Simple thinking leads him to the salvation of simple living. The apostle Paul thought about running the race; Gump just runs.

None of this would be reason for concern if *Forrest Gump* were still what it was a month ago—light summer entertainment with clever special-effects scenes. But in recent weeks the movie has gone from film to sociological phenomenon: $150 million in tickets sold, one million copies of the book in print, over 100,000 CDs of the sound track distributed, and Gumpisms ("Life is like a box of chocolates. You never know what you're gonna get") analyzed on the Internet and serving as sermon texts at liberal churches.

Forrest Gump, in short, has become one of those cult films that tell us much about contemporary culture. In *Time* magazine's summary, Gump is "all-innocent and all-powerful, the ideal guru for the nervous '90s: Forrest God." The enthusiasm this story of a sinless person generates among some Christian critics shows how far discernment and expectations have fallen.

The success of the movie is particularly revealing because it differs so radically from the novel on which it is based, *Forrest Gump* by Winston Groom. Hollywood always transforms books, and has to, but in the novel (which sold only 10,000 copies when first published in 1986) Gump develops a heavy marijuana habit, neglects his mother (who is forced into the poorhouse and cries herself to sleep every night), and becomes a professional wrestler ("The Dunce"). In the novel he ends up a transient wandering through the South, playing a harmonica and other instruments in city squares while folks throw quarters in a tin cup and sleeping with a waitress from a striptease joint.

The book, in short, shows a person who sins and needs Christ. It begins with Gump not as a naturally pure child but as one who scorns kids worse off than himself, "retards of all kinds and spasmos." It shows him in adult life not as a rock for flower child Jenny but as a rolling stone. Jenny in the book finally walks out on Gump and marries the assistant sales manager of a roofing company because *she* wants to settle down with a home and family. (In the movie, Jenny dies of a mysterious disease, apparently AIDS; in the book, she starts going to church.)

The moviemakers in essence switched the characters of Gump and Jenny, so that the person of below-normal intelligence desires marriage and other tender mercies that give long-term satisfaction, and the smarter person avoids responsibility. *Forrest Gump* the movie is Hollywood's joke on the religious right: Here's your ideal American, and he's a simpleton.

The movie also offers a treat for the religious left: an anti-competitive ethos. Both film and novel show the swift Gump recruited by football coaches, but Gump, played by Tom Hanks in the movie, is nonaggressive; in the novel he is 6'6" and 242 pounds at age sixteen and comes to enjoy running over people. In both film and novel he gains business success in the shrimping industry, but in the movie success comes by apparent chance or pagan "destiny"; in the book it comes because Gump applies what he learns and, for a while, works exceptionally hard. Reviewers have compared Gump to Don Quixote, but Don Quixote tilts at windmills; Gump, Buddhist-like, tilts at nothing.

Christians who call *Forrest Gump* a theological film are right; but the movie is a spiritual counterfeit. The apostle Paul knew the limitations of man's wisdom, but he did not substitute for it man's stupidity. He wrote that "Greeks look for wisdom, but we preach Christ crucified . . . for the foolishness of God is wiser than man's wisdom, and the weakness of God is stronger than man's strength" (1 Corinthians 1:22-23, 25). *Forrest Gump* the movie tells us that *man's* weakness is stronger than man's wisdom.

Discerning Christians, by comparing Paul and Gump, can use the movie as a springboard to evangelism. For Christians who embrace *Forrest Gump*, however, the title of a J.B. Phillips book rings true: *Your God Is Too Small.* If we desire movies that display faith in original innocence, our cultural goal will be the humanistic movies of the Production Code era and the television shows of the 1950s. But since the Bible presents the truth about original sin and God's grace, should we settle for so little?

What Breaks Your Heart?

BY MARVIN OLASKY
SEPTEMBER 10, 1994

"Ease his pain," the disembodied voice in *Field of Dreams* tells Kevin Costner. The pain referred to in that movie is the gap between father and son; it eventually is eased as they engage in a twilight game of catch. But two of the high points in Ken Burns's *Baseball* miniseries, which begins September 18 on PBS, show that it is easy to play catch at times but harder to play catch-up after years of bitterness.

One of the miniseries's emotional highs comes in the sixth show, scheduled for September 25th: its centerpiece is the integration of baseball in 1947. The episode only touches on the background, but books by Jules Tygiel and Maury Allen go deeper into the motivations of Branch

Rickey, general manager and part-owner of the Brooklyn Dodgers. The sixty-five-year-old, Bible-believing Rickey explained his decision to end a half-century of baseball segregation by saying, "I couldn't face my God much longer knowing that his black creatures are held separate and distinct from his white creatures in the game that has given me all I own."

Rickey recruited for his "great experiment" Jackie Robinson, a fine player with a hot temper. During a three-hour meeting Rickey, who had learned of Robinson's church upbringing, pretended to punch his recruit on one cheek, then gave him a biography of Jesus. Robinson evidenced no faith in Christ as an adult, but he remembered the scriptural teaching and said, "I get it. What you want me to say is that I've got another cheek."

The turn-the-other-cheek plan worked, as Robinson's perseverance in doing his job without responding to vile provocations impressed even baseball's racists. Rickey also made a big profit as Brooklyn attendance increased, and that had also been one of his motives, but Robinson wrote in his autobiography that this was fine: "I also know what a big gamble he took." Robinson's superb play helped his teammates win the pennant and get World Series dollars: White players who did not like blacks liked green.

Robinson, however, had agreed to turn the other cheek for only three years. He did so manfully but not joyfully. Once "emancipated," Robinson spoke out furiously against managers, players, and umpires during the remaining eight years of his baseball career. The abuse he had received, including numerous death threats, left Robinson so suspicious that those who did not know the full history called him paranoid. But he had real enemies.

Rickey, who emphasized performance, had said that "a baseball box score is a democratic thing." Angry at major-league baseball for its lack of black managers and general managers, Robinson saw that discrimination remained in areas not so readily measured by statistics. Even after receiving adulation throughout the 1960s, he titled his autobiography *I Never Had It Made*; it was published in 1972, the year he died at age fifty-three, full of anger and frustration. Baseball eased his pain, but—as he lived his adult life apart from the Bible—it may eventually have increased it.

The ninth and last episode of *Baseball*, scheduled for September 28, shows Robinson's funeral and notes that baseball itself was staggering until it received a lift from what Burns labels the greatest World Series game ever played, the sixth game of the 1975 series. That's the game in which a series of dramatic ups and downs concluded with an extra-inning, game-winning home run down the left field line by Boston Red Sox catcher Carlton Fisk. Since I practically grew up at Fenway Park in Boston as a teenager during the 1960s and did not become a Christian until 1976, I understand the Burns-recorded amazement of historian Doris Kearns: "The way the whole ballpark was moving with Fisk to will that ball fair . . . as if you could really make spiritual, magical things happen. And it happened."

But what happened? The organist at Fenway Park played "The Hallelujah Chorus," and "church bells rang out all across New England." Was the Red Sox triumph a spiritual experience? Burns's last episode has editor Dan Okrent saying of baseball, "It tells me there's something in the world I can count on and that is never going to let me down." Hey, baseball for a time also filled a hole in my soul, and it still has a tenacious hold on me—but get a life, guys! Ease the pain through playing catch, yes, but if we turn baseball from an ideal pastime into an idolatrous religion, the bitterness of life will keep outrunning us and we'll never catch up.

Baseball "breaks your heart," the last episode tells us, but that is an exaggeration. Baseball twisted and turned Jackie Robinson's heart, and in a lesser way it causes fans to lose sleep. But it's the American Civil War, with 600,000 deaths, or the Rwandan civil war, with even more, that breaks hearts. Or ask Baltimore Orioles infielder and baseball chapel leader Tim Hulett, whose small son died in an accident two years ago, what breaks hearts and what fixes them. Not baseball, but death, breaks hearts; not baseball, but Christ, fixes them.

Stealth Education

BY MARVIN OLASKY
FEBRUARY 25, 1995

The other night I read to beloved Benjamin, my youngest son, one of the books he had picked out at the local library. Benjamin at age four judges books by their covers, and *The Duke Who Outlawed Jelly Beans* looks good. Its cover features a boy in a crown speaking from atop a large bird as seven children of various nationalities and skin colors listen. The stories within, starting with "The Frog Prince," have good opening action and colorful pictures. Once each story is underway, though, insinuations begin to appear, and soon something unnatural this way comes: One child has two "fathers," another has two "mothers." Unlike the infamous *Heather Has Two Mommies*, a book that with its title is a set-up to be taken down, *The Duke Who Outlawed Jelly Beans* is an infiltrator, a stealth educator—and that's the way most education works.

At the beginning of this century the English journalist G.K. Chesterton pointed out that children often don't listen to what they are told, but what parents and teachers assume without saying sinks in and affects them in subtle ways. At mid-century C.S. Lewis pushed that idea forward in books like *The Abolition of Man*, wherein he showed that a grammar textbook was actually proclaiming the death of objectivity. (The text taught that when we make statements about external artifacts or events, we're really describing what we think and not what we're seeing; in other words, the grammar book was teaching that reality is purely subjective.)

Now, at the end of the century, People for the American Way overlooks liberalism's diseases and spends its time complaining about "stealth candidates": Conservative Christians who run for school boards and refuse to wear on their backsides signs that say, "I'm a religious right fanatic, kick me." But it's the stealth sapping that goes on in government classrooms and the stealth propaganda of books all the way down to the level of *The Duke Who Outlawed Jelly Beans* that deserve special scrutiny.

The stealth press is also an irritation. When super-liberal Eleanor Clift describes herself as being "in the broad middle," and PBS leftist Nina Totenberg calls herself a "lifetime moderate," I am annoyed with them not for their liberalism but for their lying. *Time* Senior Writer Margaret Carlson's comment concerning her coverage of Hillary Clinton is much better: "When you're covering someone like yourself, and your position in life is insecure, she's your mascot. . . . You're rooting for your team."

I do not mind if pro-abortion reporters march in pro-abortion parades; I'm concerned with the stealth editors who forbid reporters to march and then parade their subtle propaganda down the news pages. The open slams, such as the *Washington Post's* description of Jerry Falwell and Pat Robertson supporters as "largely poor, uneducated and easy to command," are easy to refute. I am more concerned about the stealth tactics that lead reporters to sidestep the ideas of Newt Gingrich or Phil Gramm by labeling their carriers as "mean."

Christian parents confronted by stealth have hard choices to make while raising children. We can cloister them, but children never exposed to childhood diseases are at greater risk of serious reactions when they become adults. Or we can teach children, from the time they understand that there is a world beyond their homes, that they live in a world where stealth abounds.

I'm not in favor of letting children watch inappropriate movies, but what do we do with movies that are OK except for a stealth scene or two? My sense is that we can let children watch a movie that here or there insinuates the normality of some vulgar language or conduct, but instead of letting it slide by we must indicate that such words and deeds are unacceptable to parents and to God. (This can only work if we do not talk or act that way ourselves.)

Controlled exposure of children to cultural viruses is not a happy solution, because evil ideas can roll around in brains and have dire consequences; the long-range strategy, if Christ does not come soon, should focus on recapturing the culture. But the stealth warriors are out there, and if our children do not begin to identify them while we are still by their sides, they will meet them on grounds of the enemy's choosing.

What If the Parents Shrug?

BY MARVIN OLASKY
APRIL 8, 1995

Take one baby abandoned by a crack-addicted mother and almost crushed to death in a trash truck. Add two parents who adopt that child and bond so successfully that the child, at age three, won't eat a fast-food hamburger when separated from them. A Hollywood-size happy tale, right?

Wrong. *Losing Isaiah*, the big message movie now prowling the theaters, displays not only our culture's emphasis on skin color and ambivalence about adoption, but our tendency to think that middle-class parents are camels on whom more and more straws can be loaded. But before we hit the cosmic significance of this film, let's take a quick run through the plot. I don't mind spoiling it for you, dear reader, because I am helping you save the ticket price for a worthier excursion.

Act I: Two women, both stereotyped. The dark-skinned, drug-addicted one (there's that common Hollywood equation of black life and squalor) tosses aside her tot. The light-skinned one with a flickering marriage and a back-talking teenage brat (both of those background elements are from Dial-A-Script) adopts baby Isaiah.

Act II: Drug addict turns her life around. Addicts who change usually do so through religious conversion, but this movie ignores God except when the ex-addict explains her rationale for trying to reclaim Isaiah, now three: "Look in the mirror. I'm his mother. God says so." Skin color apparently is God's message to us, although Isaiah himself doesn't see it that way. Asked by his white sister to compare her hand with his and pronounce the difference, Isaiah (in one of the movie's infrequent true-to-life moments) says, "My hand's smaller."

Act III: Judge rules for the birth mother on the basis of skin color: Isaiah "needs to know who he is." Adoptive parents accept judgment tearfully. New mom can't handle Isaiah; three-year-old, wisely imitating Gandhi, goes on hunger strike. After two weeks new mom turns in desperation to adoptive mom, and it looks like the two will raise the child together: Hurray, Isaiah has two mommies!

Epilogue: The Deeper Meaning. The movie finally recognizes the Bible by filling the screen at the end with the verse, "And a little child shall lead them." The verse (Isaiah 11:6) refers to the messianic age of perfect safety: Wolf and lamb, leopard and goat, calf and lion will be pals, and a little child will play with ferocious beasts. The movie, however, prophesies a new, progressive family structure in which middle-class parents will provide long-term foster care, and single moms living on the economic edge will be able to take over when they feel up to it.

Dumb: The National Council on Adoption has pointed out the folly of viewing adoptive parents as a resource to be exploited in this way. Children do not need the limitations of having only one parent or the confusion of having multiple variations, but rather the certainty of having a mother and a father. Parents need to know that they have responsibility and authority, or else it will become harder to find parents who will make the long-term commitment to raising hard-to-place children such as crack baby Isaiah.

Dumber: The tendency to think of parents as beasts of burden is also evident in current tax debates. Some Republican economists, arguing that the issuing of a $500 per child tax credit is of little economic value, would rather put the priority on lowering marginal rates or capital gains taxes. Those reductions would also be good, but parents should come first, unless we think they can bear any burden, pay any price, take any licking, and still keep ticking.

The shrug: The novel *Atlas Shrugged* has one of the most evocative titles in publishing history. Author Ayn Rand was an atheist with many muddle-headed theories, but she was right in her suggestion that capitalism is an economic Atlas on whose shoulders the world rests and in her question about what would happen if entrepreneurs burdened by taxes and regulations simply . . . shrugged. That's the question we need to ask today not only about adoptive parents but about all parents, and dads especially—for millions now do give up by embracing divorce or abandonment. Many parents still hang in there, but as television shows or movies ridicule fathers and mothers, and as government unnecessarily burdens and encumbers them, we need to wonder: What if they also shrug?

Studying Babylon

BY MARVIN OLASKY
FEBRUARY 24, 1996

Why have movie and television reviews at all? Why review programs or films that are not child-friendly? Why not just review evangelical films specifically made for Christian audiences? Three reasons:

God's common grace does allow some good secular productions to come into existence, and most *World* readers like to know about them.

Hollywood is still America's dream factory. Just as Daniel had to understand Babylonian culture in order to interact effectively with the rulers around him, so we must know the dreams that have become central to ours.

The Christian cultural separatist dream is dead. Walk into any evangelical church, and it is likely that most of the teens there have watched *Friends* and other hit shows; we need to know how to react.

Our task at *World*, then, must be to review major media products, or else we are not being true to the mission statement printed each week. The reviewer's job is difficult, though, because it involves not only service as the eyes and ears of our readers, but teaching discernment as well. It is always important to warn readers about violence, sexual suggestiveness, and profanity, but merely totaling up manifestations of sin is a task for an accountant, not a trainer.

Yes, Hollywood's fixation on sex must be fought, but at the same time we should note the deeper danger: Consumers of popular culture, including Christians, are often subtly conditioned to oppose transcendental reality and objective virtue.

Yes, be careful, little children, what you see, but what's more shattering than an occasional shoot-out is the common presentation of a world without religion, one in which noble thoughts are rarely uttered during prime time and even tough-guy protagonists who pretend to be men of steel are morally sad sacks of straw.

We should not attempt to be holier than God by declaring that evidence of man's depravity, which the Scriptures emphasize so emphatically, is off-limits for Christians today. That's why during the past year our film reviewer, Pam Johnson, gave two cheers to riveting but uncomfortable movies like *Braveheart* and *Rob Roy*.

We will not duck such difficult encounters, but what we really long to praise are films and programs that show how spectacular the unspectacular can be. A fine film from the eighties, *Tender Mercies*, quietly showed the sweetness of small moments, and we are celebrating this year the fiftieth anniversary of a movie that did that best of all. Director Frank Capra's *It's a Wonderful Life* (1946) delightfully depicts a type of born-again experience and also illustrates the perseverance in doing good that Christians are to have.

After all, the hero of that movie, played by Jimmy Stewart, could have done great things by worldly standards. He could have moved to the big city. He could have joined the big bank at a greatly increased salary. Yet he sticks with his tiny outfit that merely gives hard-working poor folks the opportunity to own their own homes. The film resonates with me every time I visit a good but struggling inner-city Christian poverty-fighting group and contrast it with well-funded government welfare organizations.

How many of this year's movies will be remembered fifty years from now? How many are remembered fifty days after release? Frank Capra had not only genius but a "sense of responsibility," according to novelist Graham Greene, "a kinship with his audience, a sense of common life, a morality."

Capra's films, including *Mr. Smith Goes to Washington* and *Meet John Doe*, do not move well just because he had good intentions. Since, in Capra's words, "crowd reactions are precisely what the film was made for in the first place," he taped preview showings and, listening to the tapes, noted that "when the film was interest-grabbing the audience was silent, hushed. Where it was dull or long, I heard coughs, shufflings, rattlings of peanut bags." Capra then re-edited the film to maximize interest.

Capra made movies move, and that's a feature some deeply moral films and programs lack. What's missing from most of today's bad entertainment products is a morality that overarches the minute to minute and can last a lifetime. What's missing from some films praised by evangelical reviewers for their decency is enough cough-silencing action.

Morality and movement: At *World*, we're constantly looking for products that combine the two. When we find something good, we will tell you about it in our pages. We will also critique the bad, so you can tell others how far short of true good it falls.

Environmentalism

Rats, Fetuses, and a
Knowledge of God

BY JOEL BELZ
OCTOBER 12, 1987

Poor Stanford University has a tough problem. The prestigious California school, noted again within the last month by many as the top university in America, wants to build a major new biology research laboratory. The plans are drawn, the financing is ready, but the facility is not being built.

Stanford's laboratory project is at a standstill, and has been for several months, because of the vigorous protests of some animal rights activists who are deeply concerned that the rats and other small mammals necessary for research might be misused. The university had already built one $13 million state-of-the-art lab but wanted to add a second one like it. The protesters are firmly in the way.

At risk, according to Stanford president Donald Kennedy, is important research on the immune system, cancer genetics, developmental biology, and various inherited diseases of childhood. In the battle, Kennedy has come to distrust the animal rights activists as basically dishonest. First, he says, they claim that all they want is better living conditions for the critters. Then, when such conditions are provided (at enormous expense), the activists say they oppose any injury or pain at all. And finally, they call into question all biomedical research as a failed enterprise.

Really, charges Kennedy, these folks are antiscientific. Their expressed purpose is animal rights, but they have attracted to themselves all sorts of other causes as well, including the antinuclear crowd, environmentalists of various stripes, and even—could it really be?—some prolifers concerned that the new lab might be the site of experiments using fetal tissue.

Slipping in that last group changes the story a bit, doesn't it? Until then, perhaps, you were pretty much on Dr. Kennedy's side, cheering him on in his concern to put down a senseless bunch of kooks. But are they really going to be experimenting with human fetal tissue in those new labs? Where is all of this brave new world of experimentation going to lead us?

So now, you see it's not just the animal rightists, the antinukers, and the radical environmentalists who are seen as antiscience and antidevelopment. Now you and I are in the same category, whether or not we feel totally comfortable with our "cobelligerents."

Dr. Kennedy's case, which just a few minutes ago seemed so sound, now makes us wonder. What is his reference point? Where does he anchor his value system?

What is happening, of course, is that those in the non-Christian world, the humanists who have stressed that man is the measure of all things, are increasingly demonstrating that their shallow philosophies are full of hard inconsistencies. Because first of all they are willing to deny God as Creator of all things, they have no basis now for seeing a distinction between the life of a rat, the life of a cancer cell, or the life of an unborn infant. The causes are all there for various advocates to sort through, picking whichever one seems particularly pleasing or odious.

Nor is Donald Kennedy above it all. His own personal cause (and he seems bewilderingly bewildered in defending it) is little more than an abstraction. Plaintively, he pleads for the right of "science" to move on unfettered as it charges in a hundred different directions of exploration. Never pausing to tell us whether the nation's leading university has anything thoughtful to say about how the lives of rats, cancer cells, or unborn babies are to be compared, he begs us to let them go on with their highly important scientific tasks.

Poor Stanford University. Poor Donald Kennedy. Poor educational and scientific establishment. For too long they all have shut out the God who ties it all together. They've ignored the God who created everything there is, including the rats that—because they too are God's handiwork—we will not torture even when we kill them for higher ends. The scientists have also denied the sense in which illness and disease are part of God's punishment for the very rebellion of which they are a part. And they've closed their eyes to the gracious sense in which God has singled out human beings, unique in all his creation, for a heroic rescue through the redemption of Christ. It's that very act that tells us there is a scheme of things, that some things (for example, unborn babies) are more important in God's eyes than others (for example, rats).

Until American education and American science get those things in their minds and hearts, maybe it's just as well that Stanford's new lab remains unbuilt.

Don't Scorn a Subspecies

BY JOEL BELZ
MAY 19, 1990

Red squirrels in Arizona stole the environmental limelight from spotted owls in Oregon last week—with a little help from Secretary of the Interior Manuel Lujan, who asked bluntly whether it really needs to be the federal government's responsibility to ensure the durability of "every subspecies" in the animal kingdom.

The flap came in the wake of an environmental impact study required when a $200 million National Science Foundation telescope project was proposed for Mount Graham in Arizona. The study found that a nearly extinct population of 180 red squirrels might disappear altogether if the big scope's construction were allowed to continue.

Lujan suggested in response that "nobody's told me the difference between a red squirrel, a black one, or a brown one." And he asked, "Do we have to save [an endangered species] in every locality where it exists?"

Conservationists weren't one bit happy with Lujan's remarks. Officials of the National Wildlife Federation and the Wilderness Society called them "totally outrageous" and said the secretary demonstrated an "incredible lack of understanding."

As animal rights activists become increasingly vocal in our generation, Christians have a significant contribution to make to a discussion that otherwise might get altogether out of hand. Because they take the Bible seriously, they will show up somewhere between the rabid conservationists on the one hand and the rabid utilitarian school on the other. And they will do so not merely to help bring peace, but out of strong biblical principle.

As utilitarians, Christians must insist that the genuine needs and the welfare of human beings always take precedence over the needs and the welfare of animals. God created things that way. Men and women are in God's image. Spotted owls and red squirrels (and even cocker spaniels and Arabian horses) aren't. The implication heard increasingly these days that there is some equality of interests involved must be soundly rejected— simply on the basis of God's creation order.

But that same creation order also has something to say to those who exploit and recklessly abuse the animal kingdom. It was God—not some random system of chance—who created red squirrels as well as black ones and brown ones. We have to assume that he did so not in a flippant or casual manner but for reasons we may not yet understand. And if that attitude controls our outlook, we won't get caught demeaning even a subspecies that God thought important enough to create.

Obviously, those two commitments—both springing from a confidence in a Creator God—will sometimes bump into each other, as they have now in Arizona, and as they did not long ago in the Pacific Northwest where diminished spotted owl populations are being used by conservationists to threaten significant numbers of jobs held by logging and timber workers. What happens when the two principles collide?

What happens is that we apply wisdom to the situation—not simplistic formulas. We avoid demeaning remarks about anything God has made, and we make serious efforts to preserve all his handiwork—even at the subspecies level. We might go so far as to say we won't threaten any of God's creatures just because of human whim and recreational fancy.

But whim and fancy are not the same as serious scientific pursuit and the day-to-day employment that sustains human society. When those are the issues, the orderly priorities of God's creation take over. No one knows for sure the red squirrel can't live elsewhere. We do know for sure it is biblically right to ask the creature, not the human being, to make the attempt to readjust.

The Earth Is the Lord's

BY MARVIN OLASKY
JULY 6, 1996

When our dog died recently, I had to explain to my youngest son Benjamin, five, that all dogs don't go to heaven. People have souls that never die, but dogs do not, I pointed out.

Ben, cogitating, responded, "Then people are special?" That's right, Ben, that's right—and that understanding separates true Christian environmentalists from the conventional liberal environmentalism that rules the pages of *Time* and even some Christian publications.

True Christian environmentalism begins with the understanding that the world is material, but in the world are people who have souls that never die. People, made in the image of God, are the only ultimately valuable cargo carried on Spaceship Earth.

We need to take care of our environment because it declares God's glory, because He told us to take stewardly dominion over the world, because we need its resources for our material survival, and because we love our land. I still remember bicycling across the United States from Massachusetts to Oregon twenty-five years ago and feeling the beauty of this great big country, slow mile after slow mile.

Nevertheless, we need to remember that the environment by itself is a thing, and people are far more important than things or creatures not made in God's image. Conventional liberal environmentalists often characterize themselves as anti-materialistic, but those who worship the world rather than the God who created it are actually the most materialistic of all, because what they see and prize is material.

Some Christian environmental organizations avoid outright material worship but foster the syncretizing of Christianity and materialism. Recently Richard Austin, a former Presbyterian Church (USA) pastor, gave the opening address at EarthCare '96, a Christian environmental stewardship conference in Chattanooga. Mr. Austin said, "We are used to proclaiming Christ as fully God and fully man. Christ is also fully God and fully earth, a creature of this earth. 'For God so loved the world' that he sent Jesus [is] everyone's favorite passage, but it is not just us, it is the world that is the object of love in that passage."

There's a tinny ring of truth in that statement—Christ is the second Adam, and Adam was made from the dust of the earth—but some Christian-materialist syncretism as well. After all, God is the Creator, and we are his creatures, not the earth's. "Fully earth" is not an equivalent to "fully man," unless we see man as material alone.

Crucially, the verse that follows John 3:16 goes like this: "For God did not send his Son into the world to condemn the world, but to save the world through him." The apostle John here is clearly writing about people, for the same writer records in Revelation that this material world will not be saved.

This world dies, but human beings have eternal life.

History

Containing Corruption

BY MARVIN OLASKY
AUGUST 27, 1994

While researching a book on eighteenth-century American history, I've been struck repeatedly by the parallels between Washington, D.C.'s arrogance in 1994 and London's in 1774. The centralizing economic goals of 1990s liberalism are not all that different from those that animated George III's advisers—and, as the health care and crime bill debates show, they are beginning to receive a similarly vigorous response. When British leader Charles Townshend called the American colonists "children planted by our care, nourished by our indulgence," another Member of Parliament, Isaac Barre, who had gained a scar on his face while aiding the colonies during the French and Indian War, roared in response, "They nourished by your indulgence? They grew by your neglect of 'em. As soon as you began to care about 'em, that care was exercised by sending persons to prey upon 'em." Modern entrepreneurs who are sick of Washington's "nurturing" could say it no better.

England, however, had not only a vainglorious king but a corrupt Parliament—and British political theorists such as James Burgh proposed practical improvements. Burgh's book *Political Disquisitions*, published in 1774, recommended a "rotation of offices" under which Members of Parliament would be replaced after several years' service but could come back later. Arguments against rotation were similar to those against term limits now. Burgh noted, "It is pretended by the court-party that a whole house of inexperienced members would be at a loss about the forms." But Burgh argued that those who grew accustomed to court life forgot the interests of the country; furthermore, corrupt incumbency conferred such advantage that "if the majority of the house be not changed every other year, the same men may be reelected for 20 years together."

The American colonists agreed that longevity in power contributed to unsavory legislative longings. Turnover in their colonial assemblies was desirable, they argued, because prolonged time away from constituents tempted a representative to join with other representatives in conspiring against the public. Legislators who enjoyed life in the capital more than simpler countryside pleasures also became easy prey for royal governors. Recognizing the temptations, colonists made sure that legislative posts brought with them only a pint of power and a dollop of money; legislators received no regular salaries and had to make do with a stipend for attendance that often barely covered expenses. Long sessions lost legislators money.

Burgh's recommendations so impressed John Adams that he strove "to make the Disquisitions more known and attended to in several parts of America." Americans listened to Adams: George Washington, John Hancock, and Thomas Jefferson all purchased Burgh's book. They saw in it a confirmation of the pattern the colonists had developed. Massachusetts, for example, had averaged about a 45 percent turnover per legislative session from 1700 through the Revolution and New Jersey slightly over 50 percent. In Virginia and South Carolina over half the legislators elected had stayed just one term.

Diaries during the pre-Revolutionary period show the effectiveness of such informal term limits. When Pennsylvania neighbors asked Edward Shippen of Pennsylvania to run for election, he replied that he was "not anxious to be in the House. A seat there would give me much trouble, take up a great deal of my time and yield no advantage." The response of Henry Beekman, pushed to stand for reelection to the New York Assembly, was typical: "If other good men can be fixed on, I had rather be out than in." John Adams's reaction upon being chosen a representative for the first time was not unusual. "Many Congratulations were offered, which I received civilly, but they gave no Joy to me," Adams wrote. "At this time I had more Business at the Bar, than any Man in the Province. . . . I was throwing away bright prospects. . . ."

The founding fathers could have placed a mandated rotation of offices into the Constitution, but there was no need to: The task could be accomplished unofficially by keeping pay low and governmental power minimal. Today congressional seats provide not only enormous power, big salaries, and generous perks, but a financial afterglow: Those with long service in

Congress can get well-paid jobs as state university presidents or interest group lobbyists (but I am being redundant). Opponents of term limits suggest that the founding fathers two centuries ago opposed them, since the Constitution did not establish them. However, the founders in the 1780s spent little time discussing whether to require a rotation of offices, for they did not predict a class of professional legislators.

Now that we have been surprised by the politics of permanence, term limits are needed. They should not be oversold, for they will not eliminate sin. Yet, as Burgh wrote in 1774, "The difficulty of excluding corruption is no reason for giving over all endeavors to abolish it; any more than the difficulty of living a virtuous life amid the various temptations to which our frail nature is exposed, is a reason for our giving over all endeavors to regulate our conduct."

Washington's Birthday

BY MARVIN OLASKY
FEBRUARY 11, 1995

George Washington's birthday (now multi-presidentialized) has become so much a shopping day for cards and sundries that we forget about the Continental Congress's big shopping expedition 220 years ago, in 1775. Looking for a general to fight a Revolutionary War, John Adams and company chose Washington for four reasons: He had gained a reputation as a courageous and discerning officer during the French and Indian War; he was popular among Virginians who were wondering whether they should be involved in what was seen as a New England war; he was known as an exemplary moral figure who could unite Americans principally concerned with higher taxes and those whose greatest desire was for righteous government; beyond all that, he was tall, like King Saul.

The British believed the last reason to be the only explanation for his ascendancy. They called his military strategy amateurish and made their scorn seem reasonable by sweeping Washington's army out of New York in 1776. They grew particularly sarcastic when Washington, at a time when army camps were homes for blasphemy, attacked the "foolish and wicked practice of profane cursing and swearing" and told his men that "we can have little hopes of the blessing of Heaven on our arms, if we insult it by our impiety and folly."

Sophisticated British leaders saw Washington as a backwoods Bible-thumper when he demanded the appointment of regimental chaplains, commanded his soldiers to "attend carefully upon religious exercises," and noted that "The blessing and protection of Heaven are at all times necessary but especially so in times of public distress and danger." The general the British worried about was not Washington but Charles Lee, who was professionally trained and scoffed at ideas of God's blessings. The atheistic Lee hated the church so much that he resolved not to be "buried in any church or church yard. . . . I have had so much bad company [with Christians] while living, that I do not choose to continue it when dead."

In 1776 some leading officers and politicians wanted to remove Washington from command and install Lee in his place, even though Lee was known more for his adulterous conquests of women than his victories in war. But Lee's frequent fornications finally caught up to him in December 1776 when British cavalry, told that Lee was sleeping with a woman three miles outside the camp, captured him.

The Redcoats relaxed, thinking they had seized the only competent general the Americans had, and the British commanding general, Sir William Howe, absorbed himself in adultery with his mistress, Elizabeth Loring.

Annoyed American Tories made up a ditty concerning Howe: "Awake, arouse, Sir Billy, / There's forage on the plain. / Ah, leave your little filly, / And open the campaign." But it was no use: Howe preferred his unholy pleasures, and local British commanders mimicked their leader's laziness. For example, in December 1776 Johann Rall, who commanded the Hessian forces at Trenton, did not even emphasize the posting of sentries. He said, according to testimony at British investigations later, "These country clowns cannot whip us. . . . If the Americans come, we'll give them the bayonet."

Rall also saw no reason to pay attention to urgent messages given him on Christmas Eve, 1776 because everyone knew that Washington was a wimp and the defeated Americans were slouching off in dejection. What Rall did not realize was that those men who stayed with Washington were ready to move fast and fight hard. When a Tory farmer delivered to Rall a note saying the entire American army had crossed the Delaware River during a storm and was marching on Trenton, Rall was intent on his card game and did not read the note but merely slipped it into his pocket and went on gambling and drinking. When Washington and his troops arrived early the next morning, they routed Rall's hung-over Hessians.

What elevated Washington above the British generals was not strategy but morality and tenacity. The journalist Thomas Paine, who had neither, profiled Washington late in 1776 and was astounded at Washington's single-minded perseverance: "There is a natural firmness in some minds which cannot be unlocked by trifles." Eight days after the battle of Trenton, at dusk on January 2, 1777, Lord Charles Cornwallis's army pinned Washington's forces against the Delaware River. Cornwallis, looking forward to a night of relaxation, is reputed to have said, "We've got the old fox safe now. We'll go over and bag him in the morning." During the night the American army slipped around the British left flank and was able to rout a British regiment at Princeton.

Washington's emphasis on the way virtue and liberty went together was vindicated in military contest; later, as President, he embodied the same combination.

Acting Up Among the Redcoats

BY MARVIN OLASKY
APRIL 22, 1995

April is the coolest month. Not only is the weather great over many of the United States, but April typically begins with the NCAA roundball championships, and this year will conclude with the top hardball players back on the field after their abysmal strike. This April began with a splendid tax cut conclusion to the Contract, one that allowed Republicans to go home with a shout heard across America. This week we are celebrating the 220th anniversary of the shot heard around the world.

Commemorating the start of the American Revolution—"By the rude bridge that arched the flood / Their flag to April's breeze unfurled"—resonates well in this year's political climate. Many students whose high school history courses still mention "minutemen" know that the patriots fought taxation without representation. Some scholars know that Americans also waged a culture war against lordly London's deistic tendencies.

What few people know, even as the debate about homosexuals in the military reopens, is that the success of the American military effort begun at Lexington and Concord owed much to the public and private failures of the British cabinet minister who was in charge of the war effort and was also England's most notorious homosexual.

George Sackville, a major general court-martialed for cowardice in 1759, had reemerged by 1775 as a favorite of King George III, and that year the king appointed him Secretary of State for the American colonies, with responsibility for running the military effort on land.

It was Sackville's other activities on land that untied the tongues of British gossips. In 1776 William Jackson's poem "Sodom and Onan" criticized the king for his appointment of Sackville and his willingness "To pardon Sodomites and damn the Nation. / Sackville . . . kisses hands / With lips that oft in blandishment obscene / Hath been employed." Sackville threw fuel on the fire by appointing to key positions two men also suspected of sodomy; one, New Hampshire Tory Benjamin Thompson, became undersecretary of state, and the future Marquess Wellesley complained about the power of "Sir *Sodom* Thompson, Lord Sackville's *under* Secretary."

Sackville's promotion and protection of young homosexuals made him unpopular among his cabinet colleagues. The First Lord of the Admiralty believed Thompson was selling naval information to the French and wanted to put him on trial, but Sackville protected him and, faced with "general disrespect for his person" from able officials, brought in other aides who were "of doubtful morals, and worse than doubtful integrity." Still, King George III trusted Sackville and gave him almost complete say in promoting generals and deciding on grand military strategy.

Sackville messed up in this domain, as was his custom: "Capable of rousing himself to almost frenzied pitches of energy, he habitually lapsed into periods of lethargy little better than a coma." In 1777 Sackville was so eager to get away for a weekend tryst that he sent orders to General Burgoyne in Canada to march south and have his army meet up with one marching north from New York City, but he neglected to make sure that his general in New York was informed of the strategy. The result was that Burgoyne's army, left without proper support, had to surrender at Saratoga. Reports of that big American victory convinced France to enter the war on the American side; without such support the patriots would probably have been beaten.

Following that debacle the great Edmund Burke rose in Parliament to propose Sackville's dismissal, but the homosexual official hung on, even though many talented leaders refused to work with or for him. Sackville's foolhardy military policies also made possible the British defeat that essentially ended the war. General Cornwallis was Sackville's "special favourite," and Sackville developed a southern strategy that would allow his favorite to shine. Cornwallis showed his skill by allowing his forces to be pinned in at Yorktown by American and French troops and the French navy. When Cornwallis surrendered in 1781, American independence was won.

And now, here's the moral of the story. It's not that some armed forces homosexuals cannot do a technically thorough job. But in this blessed month of April, when much seems fresh, we should keep in mind one of the laws of history: Great empires fall when their official policy, in regard to God's law, becomes "don't ask, don't tell."

History's Breathalyzer Test for Church-State Relations

BY MARVIN OLASKY
JULY 1, 1995

The Fourth of July is traditionally celebrated with fireworks that burst in air and bombastic speeches that fizzle on land. This year, as Congress debates proposals to end a third of a century of banning God from public places, and as several states plan summits of church and government leaders concerning the way of fighting poverty, we're sure to hear lots of prattle about separating church and state. Here's one thing to keep in mind in evaluating the oratory: The founders' goal was to disestablish powerful denominations without disestablishing God.

Quick history lesson: The early state constitutions were theocentric. The Maryland constitution of 1776 was typical in its embrace of Christianity but separation of denomination and state. The constitution proclaimed God's worship not to be an option ("it is the duty of every man to worship God") but noted that the particular style is up for grabs ("in such manner as he thinks most acceptable to him").

Crucially, Maryland banned any denominational establishment: No one would "be compelled to frequent or maintain any particular place of worship, or any particular ministry." Required tithing was satisfactory, however: "The Legislature may, in their discretion, lay a general and equal tax, for the support of the Christian religion; leaving to each individual the power of appointing the payment over of the money, collected from him, to the support of any particular place of worship or minister. . . ."

This system of denominational choice applied to aid to the poor as well: If the legislature passed a tax for supporting the poor, a taxpayer could have his money go to "the poor of his own denomination, or the poor in general of any particular county." Other states had similar rules. In South Carolina, taxes could be used to support churches, as long as no one was "obliged to pay towards the maintenance and support of a religious worship" not his own.

The Massachusetts constitution of 1780 emphasized toleration—"no subject shall be hurt, molested, or restrained, in his person, liberty, or estate, for worshipping God in the manner and season most agreeable to the dictates of his own conscience"—along with encouragement: "The happiness of a people, and the good order and preservation of civil government, essentially depend upon piety, religion, and morality . . . these cannot be generally diffused through a Community, but by the institution of the public worship of God, and of public instructions in piety, religion, and morality." Towns were to make "suitable provision, at their own expense, for the institution of the public worship of God"; the particular denominations could vary.

Virginia in 1784 came close to passing Patrick Henry's bill that declared Christianity, but not any particular variant, to be "the established Religion of this Commonwealth" and set up a property tax for support of Christian ministers and teachers. Each person when he paid the tax could name the religious society to which he dedicated the tax; if the taxpayer did not designate a particular organization, the tax would be applied to the maintenance of a county school.

Multiple establishment had broad support from Virginia leaders such as George Washington and John Marshall, who understood the social usefulness of biblical religion (whether or not its truth claims were acknowledged). But an odd bedfellow coalition among Baptists who favored separatism from society, "freethinkers" who wanted to knock Christianity off its social pedestal, and low-taxers who opposed any compulsory payments for religion, education, or social welfare sunk that bill.

A few years later the First Amendment enshrined the principle that there should be no nationally established denomination; states, of course, had the right to do as they wished. But if an orator 200 years ago had stood up on the Fourth of July and proclaimed that God was disestablished, those who were listening would have rushed forward to smell his breath: Consumption of corn likker was not scheduled to begin until the speechifying was done.

Thomas Scissorshands

BY MARVIN OLASKY
FEBRUARY 10, 1996

Presidents' Day pops up every year in February some two weeks after the Pennsylvania groundhog does, but I suspect we take notice only every four years, when it becomes time to choose the next honoree. There's something attractively zany about all these Washington-Lincoln wannabes tramping through the snow hoping to become heroes of a day dedicated not to governors or even Speakers of the House but only presidents.

Although the early presidential campaign was disappointing, it has improved ever since Bob Dole did his Humphrey Bogart imitation following Bill Clinton's State of the Union address, and Republicans began wondering whether they really wanted to invite friends to presidential debate parties in October if the best entertainment they could offer was a doleful matchup. Now, if only God (or his instrument, an honest press) will literally or metaphorically lengthen the noses of candidates who say they favor less government but are actually pushing to expand it, we might have an epic race.

It's a privilege, as Presidents' Day approaches, to be able to reflect on how God has rescued America time after time from erratic presidents. Thomas Jefferson is hailed in the history books as one of the great ones, but in the small and dingy White House of the early nineteenth century he sat at his desk with a pen knife and sliced from the Bible all passages that show God as not just transcendent but imminent as well. Miracles? Out. Christ's conception and resurrection? Out.

Through scoffing Thomas's production (not for publication in his lifetime) of what has become known as "The Jefferson Bible," the third president was showing that he wanted classical virtue without the theistic godstuff that he detested. Mr. Jefferson was well ahead of the populace generally, but he was pointing to America's twentieth-century liberal experiment: Can a western land with a marginalized Bible remain a good society? Can such a country maintain liberty without seeing it descend in license?

President Jefferson was aware of the dangers, but he was willing to take the gamble because he viewed worship of an active God as beneath man's enlightened dignity. George Washington was more faithful—he was always willing to bow before his Creator; but Abraham Lincoln also scoffed, until the enormity of several hundred lives lost in war through 1864 sent him into a theological convulsion. President Lincoln, just in time for his soul, may have gotten back in touch with the true presider over the universe.

Go through the lists of presidents since then, and very few, if any, could be termed spiritual giants. Most presidents since the 1930s have taken Jefferson to the extreme by keeping the Bible around but cutting out the parts that make them uncomfortable not only theologically but morally. Such scissoring has reached epidemic proportions in recent years—Bill Clinton, in both his political and personal lives, is its logical outcome. And yet God, in his merciful forbearance, carries through on his promise to withhold the flood and merely sends a little more snow into New Hampshire.

In one sense, Presidents' Day is merely the conflation of Washington and Lincoln birthday celebrations into one day useful for selling cards. Yet, I like to think of the day as one on which to remember all our presidents, including the recent failures—for when I think of the holiday in that way it becomes a holy day, one that brings God to mind, because only God can make a tree, and only God can hold together a country as rootless as ours has become.

I grew up in Massachusetts thirty miles from the New Hampshire border and became used to snow in winter and political snow jobs year round. But I also became used to summer days spent at Fenway Park, during years when the Boston Red Sox had bad teams. There always seemed to be a loud-mouthed fan behind me shouting, as the Sox fell behind, "Down the drain." That's what many pundits have been saying as they survey not only the Republican field but the fields that stretch across a troubled America. But God is not a fanatic like that. God is the presider above presidents, and only he gives us hope.

Foreign Affairs

The Real Enemy Doesn't Show on Our Radar Screens

BY JOEL BELZ
JULY 29, 1989

As I watched the grimy faces of a few of the 200,000 striking coal miners in the Soviet Union last week, I couldn't help thinking how much of their worldview I shared.

"We just don't believe the promises of the Moscow government any longer," the miners shouted angrily. But what they were finally concluding in mid-1989 was basically what I had been taught all my life: Never trust the Soviets.

For most of us, that's the way it's always been. There were the good guys and the bad guys—and the Russians, from the time we were little kids, were always the bad guys. We always worried that they were coming to get us.

Is that changing? The news every day provides some reason to think so. It's tough at least to argue with the new openness of the Soviet media. What we're seeing day after day would have been unthinkable half a dozen years ago.

Even so, our memories, if they are at all instructed by twentieth-century history, suggest plenty of reasons to be suspicious. And the recent quick reversals from hope to bloody carnage in China tend to dampen our expectations.

Still, as Christians we should hardly be surprised if God chooses—

anytime he wants—to rearrange the dynamics of the world political scene. He hardly owes the "good guys" anything.

Mind you, I don't go for what some people call the "moral equivalence" argument. I'm not saying that because the United States has some major blots on its record there's no difference between the U.S. and the U.S.S.R. There's a huge difference.

But a perfectly holy and a perfectly just God still would be quite vindicated if he decided to wake us Americans (and other Westerners) up a bit by saying something like this: "Now you watch while I take that big Communist bogeyman that you have so much feared all your lives and just make him disappear from the scene. Just how much better off do you think the world at large is going to be? Just how much better off do you think the U.S. will be?"

The fact is, of course, that our root problem is not really a threat from the Soviet Union. The Communists could disappear tomorrow from the Defense Department's radar scope, and our big problems would remain.

So God might well continue by saying, "Just suppose I take away the threat of the Communists. For good measure, I'll also quiet down Qadafi, I'll stop the kidnappings in Beirut, and I'll wipe the Sandinistas off the Nicaraguan map.

"So are you kidding yourself into thinking everything will be OK then? Do you Americans think you could start balancing your budget then? Keep your marriages together? End your drug problem? Bring an end to abortion? Care for your homeless? Encourage youngsters to love their parents—and parents their children?

"Or are you satisfied that with all the big-time enemies out of your way, your own wrestling with personal temptation would be any easier?"

Pogo was right. We have met the ultimate enemy, and he doesn't look a lot like Mikhail Gorbachev flying a MIG. Disturbingly, the enemy looks a whole lot more like the person we get a glimpse of every morning in the mirror.

But it may take some startling developments in world politics to persuade us of that.

View from the Back: The Whole World Needs a Message of Grace

BY JOEL BELZ
FEBRUARY 29, 1992

Flying in the economy section of a modern jetliner is no great hardship. No hardship, that is, until you glance ahead and notice the folks flying first class.

En route to Tokyo a few days ago, I was marveling at the speed, ease, and comfort with which we hurtled northwest from Los Angeles. For my wife and me, economy class was economical indeed, since it came free of charge from USAir in exchange for 100,000 Frequent Flier points. We did have to pay the $12 airport fee at Los Angeles, but for that All Nippon Airways gave us two comfy seats to Tokyo, adequate leg room, good Japanese food including sushi, a passable movie, CNN news, and a blanket and pillow.

With only twelve hours to compare our passage to that of those who tossed across the Pacific to Yokohama's port two generations ago, we should never have thought of complaining. And I don't think I did consider it until noticing the extra care lavished on the people just a few feet ahead. They ate off china and drank out of glass goblets, and I'm sure their chopsticks were lacquered. Their trays were wider, their seats plusher, their leg room longer, and they had personal TVs at each seat.

The envy I tried to repress is, I think, something like what's going on right now between the U.S. and Japan. Both societies are streaking to the end of the twentieth century with speed and comfort unimaginable to their own people when the war between them ended, and still unthinkable to most people on earth.

But the very proximity of our two societies as we speed along in our prosperity makes us edgy about each other. We covet each other's well-being. We want the very best life has to offer, and we are a little miffed if someone else gets the best before we do.

Embarrassingly, this may be hardest for us Americans. We are so accustomed to our No. 1 ranking on so many fronts that we find it hard ever to accept the reality that another nation has outdone us. Even at the

Olympics, we can't adjust to having little Norway earn more medals than we do.

Yet it is not at all a bad thing for the U.S. to have to learn to think in such ways. For us to be compelled now to look at countries such as Japan and Germany with the same eyes much of the world has had to look at us is healthy. The U.S., to be sure, has a long record of generosity toward others (not least toward Japan and Germany), but even that generosity has sometimes been administered with a combination of arrogance and clumsiness. The result is that the people back in the economy section of the plane neither love nor understand those who are flying first class.

The ultimate problem is that neither the first class passengers nor those who have economy tickets—whoever it is who fits the descriptions in this little metaphor—have a clue anymore why they are even privileged to fly in the first place. All of them are like the folks God referred to in Deuteronomy 8:17, who boasted, "My power and the strength of my hands have produced this wealth for me." Even America's generosity turns to chaff because we thought that wealth was ours to give rather than proclaiming it as a gift of God.

The nations of the world have plenty of pride. Pride leads to insults, to trade tariffs, to racism, and to shooting wars. All of those are too much for us.

What the nations of the world need right now is the message of grace. It helped me, as I sat in the economy section, to remember that I had gotten my tickets for nothing.

For Haitians, As for Christians, Grace Should Be the Theme

BY JOEL BELZ
JUNE 6, 1992

Tired of world problems that seem to have no answers? Then take on the Haiti refugee problem. The answers may not always be simple, but they're certainly clear.

I'm serious. Those of us who want to apply a biblical perspective to public affairs may find ourselves struggling sometimes with just how to go about it in specific situations. What does the Bible say about an additional $8 billion for NASA? What does it tell us about whether to check off the $1 item on the IRS form to provide funding for presidential elections? What does the Bible say about how soon the FDA should permit the unrestricted sale of genetically-engineered vegetables?

On those questions, and a million others like them, there's plenty of room for disagreement.

But on the issue of Haitian refugees, how can anyone read the Bible and not respond immediately: Open the door—wide!

If there is one thing all Christians should understand, it is the message of grace. "Freely you have received," Jesus says, "freely give" (Matthew 10:8). Who among us deserved our freedom in the first place? But now to have drunk so deeply of its blessings as most of us have in this country, and then to be grudging in extending those same opportunities to others, turns us all into ingrates of the most ignominious sort.

The biblical pattern is unmistakable. Exodus 22:21 says bluntly: "Do not mistreat an alien or oppress him, for you were aliens in Egypt." Whatever other arguments might be thought of, only one really counts— the recollection of grace in our own lives.

One reason our own age gets so tangled up on issues like this, of course, is that we get mired down in arguments about "rights" when we ought to be focusing on "grace." Yes, even aliens and refugees have rights. Leviticus 24:22 reminded the Israelites "to have the same law for the alien and the native-born. I am the LORD your God."

But there are times—and this is one of them—when discussions about rights and justice, important as they may be in other contexts, lose their relevance. Desperation calls for grace, unrestrained and plenteous.

Can it possibly matter whether the hundreds of Haitians have sat down to work out in detail whether they are "economic" or "political" refugees, to use the distinction of the Bush administration? Did your great-great-grandparents from England and Germany and Italy and Ireland have that all worked out? Or did they simply have their eyes set on the lady in New York's harbor who kept calling, "Give me your tired, your poor, your huddled masses yearning to breathe free . . ."? What makes the Haitians so different that we should now be using our military force to snuff out their small candles of hope?

No room for the Haitians? That too is a sham. The United States remains one of the least densely populated nations on earth. Only our own greed allows us to suggest such an argument.

Perhaps it's fitting that a society that has lost its way in so many other respects should now lose it as well with reference to the outstretched hand that has virtually been a national symbol since our founding.

But Christians, of all people, should speak their outrage. If we can get upset, and then organize our anger, over abuses by the National Endowment for the Arts and about the outlawing of prayerful expression in public schools, then for sure we should be raising a public witness over the current abuse of the Haitians. Rarely are biblical principles more clear.

"The LORD watches over the alien," the Psalmist reminds us, "and sustains the fatherless and the widow" (Psalm 146:9). If it doesn't bother us that official U.S. policy has increased the number of the fatherless and widows in Haiti in recent months, we should at least take note of the end of the verse: "but he frustrates the ways of the wicked."

Beware Easy Formulas

BY JOEL BELZ
APRIL 2, 1994

It would be nice if there were clear-cut tests to administer in deciding who your international friends are. There are such formulas, you know—like the one that says a little too cutely, "The enemy of my enemy is my friend." But you don't have to be too experienced in foreign policy—or any kind of human relations, for that matter—to know that you can get into big trouble if you follow such formulas formulaically.

Here's a practical example growing out of discussions we've been involved in this past week. In the Communist country of China, there's a whole structure of government bureaucracy devoted to religious affairs. Loosely related to that structure is a publishing unit known as the Amity Foundation. Amity, believe it or not, sponsors the printing and distribution of thousands of Bibles every year in different parts of China.

Sound good? On one level, of course, it is wonderful. Who can argue with the distribution of Bibles in a Communist country, especially when it's happening under quasi-government sponsorship? And even if it's only a drop in the bucket compared to the actual need, by itself it's still a good thing.

But then suppose that such an arrangement becomes the very excuse for allowing no other Bibles into the country. "Amity is meeting the need," the government says in effect. "We want this all done in an orderly way. So no one else needs to bother about Bible printing and distribution. In fact, if you do, you'll be breaking the law."

So is Amity a friend or a foe? Add to the mix a new development. Someone you know has influence with the powers-that-be at Amity and beyond and is able to twist arms so that next year Amity distributes twice as many Bibles as they did this year—all with government sponsorship. Is that good or bad?

We all need to admit that so much of our perspective depends on who we are. If you're an American businessman with a million appliances to sell to the huge Chinese population, too much preoccupation with human rights issues is nothing but a nuisance. But if, on the other hand, you're a policy-maker for the United Nations human rights commission, you find it hard to believe that decreased trade really weakens a dictator's power.

Yet you don't have to be operating in the context of foreign policy to confront such questions. For example, do you consider *The Washington Times*, with its Moonie ownership, a friend or a foe?

The pro-life movement has similarly reminded us how easy it is to find yourself walking down the street in a group including evangelical Protestants, Roman Catholics, Jews, Mormons, and perhaps even members of black Muslim groups. Who's the friend and who's the foe? And if you find yourself broad enough to accept all those folks as an appropriate alliance for this specific cause, will you also include representatives of a group called Gays and Lesbians for Life who sent us a news release last week?

Jesus could have included, if he had wanted to, a short passage in the Sermon on the Mount or in his other teachings that would have given us just the formulas we need for the occasions when we need to sort out the good guys from the bad guys. He could have distributed checklists so that the disciples could have answered fifty questions about anybody, added up the score, and put them in the right category.

You might even guess he was heading in that direction when he said in Luke 11:23, "He who is not with me is against me." But as usual, he was challenging the disciples to engage in a little more thinking than a fill-in-the-blanks sort of game would suggest. For just a bit earlier, in Luke 9:50, he also said bluntly, "For whoever is not against you is for you."

Got that one figured out?

Much of the time, Jesus' teaching is crystal-clear. But there are also many times when he seems deliberately enigmatic, appearing to encourage us both cautiously and modestly to think our way through various issues. Especially when we want to find simple ways to cut people off, or to show how good we are compared to someone else, he has a great tendency to slow us down. "Let him who is without sin cast the first stone," he says, reaching deep down into our consciences (John 8:7).

That's not because he thinks all ideas are equal and that all values are relative. God doesn't look at American freedom and Chinese dictatorship and say casually that both of them are exactly alike to him.

But God does know our great tendency toward self-righteousness. We have an uncanny propensity for a kind of historical revisionism that suggests that we, rather than God, invented human rights.

Jesus wants us to be properly valiant for the truth. He also wants us to remember that his truth was here before we were.

Broken Beyond Repair

BY JOEL BELZ
MARCH 11, 1995

Can a culture or a nation be broken beyond repair? India might be a good place to test the thesis. A five-hour bus ride from Delhi to Agra last week reminded me of all the reasons I might be tempted to say that yes, a country can be devastated beyond hope.

I had visited India briefly in 1972, carrying away two vivid memories: a terrifying 150-mile taxi ride to a city north of Delhi, and a sense of great depression because of the massive scope of the problems evident even on a quick visit. As I returned last week, I wondered whether the years had embellished my memories. Had it really been that bad?

It had been that bad. In some ways it seems even worse now.

This time, my terrifying ride took me south of Delhi instead of north, and it was by chartered bus instead of by taxi. If India's steel industry has fallen on hard times, it's because the whole annual output goes to stiffen the hearts of its drivers. Each of the 214 kilometers we traveled brought one more stomach-flipping maneuver calculated to avoid a crash only at the last split-second. Once I indeed blacked out momentarily from the certainty of a head-on crash I still think had to have occurred.

My seatmate, Mike Cromartie, and I, having staked out the front right—and therefore most dangerous—seats, laughed the forced laughs of teenage boys trying to pretend nothing was wrong. But this was no amusement-park illusion. The carcasses of big lorries, burned-out buses, and twisted farm tractors strung alongside and even across the roadway reminded us this was in fact a perilous place to be. Our lives were literally at risk.

But not nearly so much at risk, I thought, as the lives of 880 million Indians who ride and walk those same roadways every day of their risk-filled lives. If death by motor vehicle is fifty times more likely in India than in the United States (I intend to look up the statistic when and if I get home), the highways are still just a symbol of a people intent on putting themselves in harm's way.

For this road—this main highway from the Indira Gandhi International Airport to the city of the fabled Taj Mahal, this road you'd think a proud people would want to keep attractive—is lined by filth. Your choice is between the risks of staying on the road and the risks of getting off. Rotting garbage and refuse and animal waste and human sewage lie on and run down the shoulders.

I got five shots and two malaria pills before I came to India, more than for any of the trips I've made to several dozen countries. Now I wonder: How many of those shots were made necessary because of India's incredible reverence for cows? I have cleaned out barn stalls and scooped the muck from cattle trucks, so I'm not overly squeamish. But when you see a striking teenager carrying what must be thirty pounds of almost fresh cow mature on a platter just above her beautiful Indian face, you've got to wince. People everywhere fear the punishments of their gods, but sometimes the punishments they inflict on themselves are unspeakably worse.

Not far from the young woman bearing dung patties, a middle-aged man urinates openly into a scum-filled surface stream, even as two toddlers use battered aluminum pans to scrape the moistened dirt at the water's edge into a little mound.

Even if all India's traffic could be controlled, of course, and all its street-side filth swept away, horrendous problems would remain. What about a 50 percent illiteracy rate? What about thousands of eight- and nine-year-olds working in India's factories? What of an electrical supply that gets interrupted once or twice a day? What of a thirty-minute delay during the bus trip while the driver hassles the police over a border tax? And on and on.

But happily now, our bus turns safely into the paved drive amid the trimmed lawns of our hotel. Would that all India's roads led so easily after just five hours to a carpeted room with hot running water and a flush toilet. Just outside the hotel door, a live cobra and a mongoose do their thing for just 50 rupees (that's $1.50)—but unlike the rest of India, the risks there are all staged.

I need this respite. It takes a toughness I'm discovering I don't have to stare at all this brokenness and blindness and disarray at point-blank range, hour after hour, day after day. My American-style Sheraton room fits me very well, thank you, but I wonder how long it will take India, totally committed at last to major economic reform, to catch up to the United States. For now, the acute poverty rate here is higher than in any major country of the world. Is even God's great power big enough to rescue people as desperate as this?

No, neither India nor all the other developing countries of the world have a corner on brokenness. As we walk within view of the Taj Mahal—probably the most costly wedding gift in human history—my friend tells me of still another broken marriage among colleagues back home. Nor is India's awful filth the only kind, or even the worst, as I'm reminded while flipping channels on my room's television. Whatever we exported here over the last 200 years, our best-known export now may be MTV.

That's enough to depress a fellow 12,000 miles from home—except that Jesus said it wasn't whole and clean people who have need of him. It's the broken and the dirty he came to save.

Poverty Profiles

The Right Kind of Envy

BY MARVIN OLASKY
OCTOBER 28, 1995

One of my children's favorite movies is a hilarious Western parody called *The Three Amigos*. It contains no obscene language, but it does have an insulting reference to some bad guys, who are called "scum-sucking pigs." The beloved Benjamin, now five years old, stumbled on a theological truth the other day when he quoted from the movie in a way that made sense to him. "Thumb-sucking pigs," he said with a laugh.

I like that usage, even though those of us who took public school biology know that what separates pigs from human beings is the porkers' lack of an opposable thumb. "Thumb-sucking pig" is a good way of describing what we are like when envy rules our lives. We want what we do not have, and instead of working for it with our own hands, we self-absorbedly suck our thumbs and wallow in our slop, hoping to be given what we have not earned.

Calvin Trillin, author of the funny food book *American Fried*, praises the role of envy when ordering in restaurants. Do not study the menu or listen to a waiter's prattle, he writes; instead, see someone at an adjacent table eating a steak with great joy, point at him and his food, and tell the waiter, "I want some of that." The Bible is less bullish on envy, however; Hebrew and Greek words for *envy* appear twenty-three times, and twenty-two of the usages are negative.

There is one positive use: The apostle Paul in Romans 11:14 hopes that he "may somehow arouse my own people to envy and save some of them." Last week's march in Washington provided multimillions of dollars of free publicity to the Nation of Islam and probably prompted some envy among onlookers, but man-made religions cannot bring salvation and end up being destructive in this life as well. Christians need to arouse nonbelievers to constructive envy by showing through love that the Gospel turns around lives on earth and by proclaiming with credibility that it leads to eternal life in heaven.

Look, for example, at how God used Christians to help change the life of one black man, forty-one-year-old Jerry Minor. Mr. Minor started using heroin and cocaine when he was nineteen; over the next few years he turned from "recreational user" into a drug-focused wreck of a man. Minor sold drugs on the streets but did not net much cash in the process, "because I was using as much as I was making. Most of the money went right back into my body."

Minor did some jail time for drug-selling. He sometimes stayed at government-funded homeless shelters and treatment programs with the hope of stomping on his habit. But he found there "a lot of the same things that I was always doing. A lot of drugs, a lot of fights." Not until he walked into the Washington, D.C., Gospel Mission in 1992—out of desperation, not belief—did his life begin to change. "I started seeing other people accepting the Lord, and realized they were getting better. I wanted some of that, because I had tried everything else. And it was the grace of God that finally did it."

Three years and a lot of constructive envy later, Minor is working as a drug counselor at the Gospel Mission. He does not have the classroom hours that would allow him to be licensed by the government. But he knows the tricks of the drug trade and isn't easily taken in by scams; he's stood up to bullies before and isn't easily possessed by fear; he's learned to live with little and isn't readily subject to greed.

Constructive envy of the kind that possessed Minor does not occur when homeless men are thrown together into a shelter that treats them as if they did not have souls and opposable thumbs. What reached out to Jerry Minor at the Gospel Mission was love and challenge that crossed the lines of class and race and obvious sin. When Christians do not provoke constructive envy, urban warriors turn to a Farrakhan, not realizing that the paths away from Christ are those of *destructive* envy.

Constructive envy can grow only when Christians become both hearers and doers of the Word. Organizations such as CUTS and the Gospel Mission proclaim the Gospel in words that are coupled with love, so that the hurting and the lost say with Jerry Minor, "I want some of that." Many Christians talk about racial reconciliation, but if we do not pray for it and work for it, we ourselves are self-absorbedly envying a complete meal. We ourselves are thumb-sucking pigs.

Unwrapping the Gifts of the Sixties

BY MARVIN OLASKY
NOVEMBER 25, 1995

It's still trendy on the Christian left to link homelessness with supposed government cuts in social services. Nattering about Newt in the mid-nineties has replaced the roaring about Reaganism that characterized the early eighties, but the message is the same: Budget dips sink ships. The truth is different: Many of the lives sinking in recent years had holes cut into their hulls twenty-five years ago, during liberalism's golden age.

Take as a case study the story of Rudy Jones, forty-five. He grew up in a middle-class household in Washington, D.C., and as a teenager reacted, sixties-style, to school "regimentation." He became a voracious reader of political thrillers and worked for Hubert Humphrey's campaign in 1968. Then he went to college, where drugs were more important than studies, and learned about LSD, speed, and surrealistic painting.

After college Mr. Jones moved to Los Angeles and "tried to get into the film business. That's where I really got into some fast circles. I was doing a lot of powdered cocaine out there." The infantilized gratification-seeking that characterized late-sixties politics and culture stayed with him as he moved back to Washington and worked at a television station as a production technician and then as a film and tape editor.

By 1984 Cal Ripken, Jr., thirty miles to the north, had already begun his streak of showing up for work day after day, but it was hard for a child of the sixties to be an iron man. A stripper in a strip-tease joint in 1984 introduced Jones to crack cocaine, which he had heard of before as a drug that led middle-class people to "sell their houses and break up their lives."

He had scoffed at such reports, but when he took his first hit, "the bells were going off in the center of my brain."

Jones had learned during the sixties to satisfy his impulses, and he spent the mid-eighties turning theory into practice. More cocaine, more disintegration in his life: "It was like a slow-motion train wreck. A big long pile-up." Unable to work consistently because of his drug use, Jones left his job in 1988 and began a series of freelance assignments that would give him the money for crack without the obligation of regular labor.

The culmination came in September 1994 when he received a check for $1,500 from a public television station: "I just went nuts. Didn't sleep or eat for four days in a row, doing crack all the time. That's when I realized I needed to do something drastic." Drastic for Jones was entering a live-in, anti-addiction program at the Gospel Mission in a rundown area of Washington.

Ironically, it was sixties reasoning—don't think about right and wrong, just show me where I can get a buzz—that led him into a program built on right and wrong. Jones based his decision to enter the Gospel Mission not on faith in Christ, but on research showing that religious anti-addiction programs are more successful than others: "I wanted to get results, I didn't care how."

Pragmatism changed to awe as Jones went through the Gospel Mission's Bible studies and counseling programs, however. The transformation, he says, began when he stopped thinking of God as "a bunch of physics laws" and started to see him as "a personal entity that man could relate to." Suddenly he could pray, for he knew God was listening. Suddenly there was purpose that went outside self-pleasing, for God was watching. Suddenly there was power to change, because God was helping.

After five months Jones felt "completely changed." When I interviewed him in February 1995, he spoke of no longer living for each day's pleasures, as he had done since the 1960s, but dying to self—seeing God rather than man as the center of things.

Complete changes sometimes short-circuit; time heals all wounds and also tests all spiritual swoons. I've checked on Rudy Jones. He stayed clean and was judged ready to move out of the Gospel Mission in order to live with and care for his mother, who is now in her eighties and in need of help. He's working in telecommunications and volunteering twice a week to teach English and writing to newcomers at the Mission. Stuck in the sixties for three decades, he has finally grown up. And it's time that the apologists for infantilism do so also.

Dooby-Dooby-Doers

BY MARVIN OLASKY
FEBRUARY 3, 1996

Georgetown University has turned out some distinguished alumni, includ-ing the current president. But it also had the most distinguished philo-sophical exchange I ever have seen on the wall of a lavatory stall. First writer: "To be is to do." Second writer: "To do is to be." Third writer: "Dooby dooby doo."

The Bible is more straightforward: Since we are known by our fruits, we are what we do, and we are to be doers of the Word—not just hearers, certainly not just talkers. American citizenship has been weakened by our tendency to hear about problems and, instead of acting on them ourselves, turn to government. American politics has become even more suspect in recent months as oldline liberals talk about helping children while pro-moting the same old welfare dooby-dooby-doo that has done so much harm.

To meet someone who is a doer and not just a hearer and orator, jour-ney to the poor area of southeast Washington that the tourist guides for-get, Anacostia. There, in a rundown community center in the late afternoon, you might see fifty children from five to fifteen, some once-a-week volunteers, and one wiry black woman wearing a beret: Hannah Hawkins, fifty-five, a retired school administrative aide and the widowed mother of five grown children.

Mrs. Hawkins is not a fan of more federal spending that supposedly goes for children. "Oh, there's lots of government money floating around Anacostia," she says with barely-controlled anger. "I look at the budgets and I see la de da administrative cost, 85 thou a year. Assistant to the assis-tant, 60 thou a year. Services, null and void."

Mrs. Hawkins is a feisty person who keeps walking around her build-ing and gets the partly-parented children in her free-of-charge afterschool program to settle down and start on their homework. She knows each of her lambs by name, and the children know her. One sixth-grader reports getting good grades, and Mrs. Hawkins says, "Go ahead, girl." One junior-high boy makes a threatening remark to another, and the steely-eyed woman who has lived in Anacostia for over four decades reminds him quietly, "People who pick fights end up either dead or in jail."

Throughout 1995, as some private charities warned that without government funding the milk of human kindness would dry up, Hannah Hawkins persevered—and she still does. No government funds. No big donors. No blue-ribbon board of advisers. Instead, Mrs. Hawkins gleans food, books, and shoes from local businesses and churches, and she is unabashed when phone calls come in: "Excuse me. Children of Mine. Yes, I need me some dough, re, me." Glancing at some financial records, she adds, "We are flying on a wing and a prayer. Tell your neighbors to wake up little Susie."

What Hannah Hawkins will not take is a place in the jostling line of government grantees who "say they help the needy but are really the greedy." She tells of money-flush but program-poor organizations asking her to bring several dozen children on particular days when federal funders were around, so fatcat facilities wouldn't look like ghost towns: "When I first started, I used to go because I didn't know nothing. Now I'm well seasoned. I see the pimping of these children, and I will not have any part in it."

That Hannah Hawkins is no pimp is evident as she stops one child who is running by and asks, "Do you have homework?" "Yes, ma'am." "Then sit down. We can't have you running back and forth, can we?" "No, ma'am." The program is called Children of Mine because Hannah Hawkins insists that social progress comes not when professionals take on needy children as clients, but when ordinary people treat the semi-abandoned children of others as their own.

Two little children come in the front door by themselves, in time for dinner, walking past the druggies and hookers outside on Mount View Street (but there's no mountain in view), and Mrs. Hawkins gives them instructions in table manners and prayer. A strong Christian belief underlies Hannah Hawkins's willingness to serve and keep serving: "Without Jesus you're empty. You're just out to sea, floating, and don't know where to go."

For the current residents of the White House, speeches about helping children may be their last refuge. But Hannah Hawkins says she would rather be where she is than hanging out at the White House across town. "The impression you make there means nothing. But your impression here is everlasting."

From Addiction to Employment

BY MARVIN OLASKY
MARCH 23, 1996

This month the *New York Times* and Pat Buchanan—strange bedfellows—have shone spotlights on the dilemmas of workers displaced by economic change. But there's another war for jobs being waged not far from the Capitol in Washington, a war fought one soul at a time, and so far it has received little publicity.

A report on this war should begin with a look at one of its generals, Marsh Ward. Eight years ago Mr. Ward came to Washington, D.C., to build a haven for homeless alcoholics and addicts. He set up his detox program to have no rules ("they're all adults, aren't they?") and no pressure to prepare for a job ("nothing good available under capitalism anyway").

Eight years later the program run by Ward and a partner, Julia Lightfoot, is called Clean and Sober Streets, and those who enter it have a different set of rules and expectations: One strike (drinking, fighting, doing drugs, coming in late) and you're out. Don't think of yourself as a victim. When you're clean and sober you can get a job.

What happened to change Ward's thinking? He spoke softly while padding past the curtained cubicles where recent addicts lay: "Back in 1988 we believed that if you brought people in off the streets and gave them food, they'd pull themselves together and get on with their lives." But after a year he realized, "If you treat them that way, you're killing them. You're enabling them to stay with their disease." Ward also was troubled by the drug dealers who infested his rule-free program: "They could deal all day, then come back here for a room and hot meal, get their food stamps and welfare, then go back out and deal the next day."

Soon, to protect residents who did want to beat their addictions, Ward established rules: "Real simple: No violence, no sex. If you sit down, get too comfortable, make no progress, you're out. Any stealing, you're out. No alcohol, no drugs—not even legal ones, unless I've approved them. If you miss the curfew by one minute, you're out."

At first Ward's tendency was to accept excuses for violations: "We did it sometimes out of sympathy because we liked the guy—but it never worked out. Every time we let someone get by, he screwed up again. It's hard to kick people out, but you have to think of the effect on the honest people."

One of the lines of the Lord's Prayer—"Lead me not into temptation"—explains why Ward examines every prescription his residents receives: "Doctors have no sense when it comes to this group. They'll give you stuff that will get you high. Just today I told a guy to leave. He's on Paraflex, the muscle relaxant. We went to his locker today, got the bottle. He had taken fifty-five of them in the last two days. And now he's out. That's what we mean. He's an addict. And if it helps you to relax and feel good, you'll take more than is prescribed. So we play hardball."

Walks through Clean and Sober Streets show that law and order has taken over what once was a human zoo. Interviews with many of the eighty residents show they welcome the hardball approach and are ready to report on rulebreakers. ("This program is saving my life. If someone messes it up, I have no hesitancy going to the office and telling them about it.")

Ward remembers that when the program began, "there was a snitch mentality because a lot of these guys had been in prison. They wouldn't talk. Now, they feel a part of this society." And that carries over to the world outside the Clean and Sober walls: Graduates of the program have responsible jobs and are building families.

That the capitalist world is not so bad has also been a revelation for Ward: "I've found that this society has a place for everyone who is sober and responsible, who has a skill and is willing to work. No problem."

One definition of a neoconservative in politics is, "a liberal mugged by reality." Ward's experience is similar: "Yes, there's racism and injustice. But, on the other hand, if I take a guy from outside, sober him up, teach him how to read, and teach him the computer, there's a hole in the wall for that man. He goes right through."

His Eyes Have Seen the Folly

BY   M A R V I N   O L A S K Y
A P R I L   6 ,   1 9 9 6

This week, as a new season began at the Colorado Rockies ballpark in downtown Denver, junkies and winos on Larimer Street two blocks away were also celebrating the coming of spring. They had somehow survived the winter and will now once a month be able to celebrate "Christmas Day"—the day government checks arrive—by going on drinking or injecting sprees without concern about freezing to death.

The government-subsidized homeless shelters interspersed among the bars and liquor stores on and around Larimer merely enable alcoholics and addicts to remain in their state of sin and misery. But there is a better choice: Step 13, the privately-funded creation of Bob Cote, a fifty-year-old, 6-foot-3-inch ex-amateur boxer who lived on the streets in 1982 and 1983, drinking a half gallon of vodka for lunch.

Through Christ's love Cote became disgusted with what he had become; he poured out the contents of his bottle and began pouring what he had learned on the streets into a program that would challenge rather than coddle those who for too long had been seen as helpless. He worked and gained support to create a shelter where residents make their beds, cook their own meals, clean up afterwards, attend Bible studies, and submit to random urine screens and breathalyzer tests.

Now, after more than a decade of changing lives rather than providing small change, the step-by-step approach of Step 13 has proven its effectiveness. Residents who have sobered up start out at minimum-wage manual labor. Soon they can move on to positions with much higher pay at local businesses that have come to trust Cote's judgment. Residents are required to have bank accounts so they learn how to save; those who are alcoholics must take Antabuse, which produces nausea if alcohol is consumed. Step 13 understands the depravity of man.

As residents progress in work, their living conditions inside can also improve. Step 13 has eating facilities and a chapel for all to use, but the three floors of sleeping areas are highly differentiated. Residents over a year move from dormitory barracks to semiprivate and private rooms; on the way they acquire furniture and telephone accounts. When they are ready to leave, they know how to do everything that goes into having an apartment.

Step 13 costs about $3,000 per man annually, one-fifth of what it costs to keep a person for only twenty-eight days in some fancy detox centers. Residents pay about half of that from their wages, and donations take care of the other half. No government funds are used, and Cote is always on the lookout for entrepreneurial opportunities. This year he is starting up behind the shelter a car care business, so Rockies fans can park their vehicles in a secure yard before the game and have Step 13 residents shine, wax, and clean them over the next three hours.

Step 13 is still far east of Eden. One of every three of the lowest of the low—the hard-core drunks, druggies, and drifters who stagger in from Larimer Street—comes out of Step 13 clean and stays that way, able to move on to the building of careers and families. Two-thirds flunk out. But a recent study by the inspector general of the Department of Health and Human Services showed that ninety-nine of 100 alcoholics and addicts who receive government benefits fail to recover or get a long-term job.

The benefit many addicts and alcoholics like best is Supplemental Security Income (SSI), which Mr. Cote calls "suicide on the installment plan"; he has documented how SSI checks are still mailed to homeless individuals' standing accounts at liquor stores. When disability checks are sent to those who daily disable themselves, government becomes Dr. Kevorkian on a grand scale. Nor is it compassion, Cote says, to "give a street drunk a bed and a meal and some money. He knows how to work the system too well. You've got to get him out of his addiction."

Cote's eyes have seen the folly of the coming of the state. His brain and hands, through God's grace, have opened up a truly new season for hundreds over the years. Expand the Cote approach to other cities, eliminate the government's "Christmas Days," and the lives of tens of thousands would be turned around. It can be done. As a sign at Step 13 proclaims, "The day you stop making excuses, that's the day you start a new life."

Christian Conduct

Hugging the Center Line

BY JOEL BELZ
JUNE 6, 1988

Hugging the center line is a perilous way to drive. Yet that is precisely what evangelicalism is being called on constantly to do. For too many of us these days, holding uncompromisingly to a position—almost any position at all—has become embarrassing and a sure sign of narrow-mindedness.

Two influential groups within evangelicalism need to examine especially carefully their responsibility for promoting the habit of hugging the center line. Both academia and the media tug us regularly in such a direction.

Note well: I'm not referring to non-Christian institutions of higher learning or the so-called liberal media. I'm talking about the schools and the publications we've created ourselves and voluntarily support with our own money. Even these opinion-shapers constantly encourage us to trim off the sharp edges of our thinking processes.

I'm concerned that in trimming off those sharp edges we might also be saying good-bye to the cutting edge.

Colleges and universities on the one hand and the media on the other bear great responsibility for calling us to be more "open-minded" on matters such as the origin of man and the world around us, social behavioral patterns including sexual mores, issues such as patriotism and national-ism, and explanations of economic structures. The move from "right" to "left" on all these issues is historically much more likely to spring from the society's intelligentsia than from its grass roots.

By itself, of course, that proves nothing. In terms of what is biblically right and wrong, grass-roots folks are no more likely than the eggheads to be right. But the direction of the flow of ideas is worth noting—and it is a direction as true of the Christian community as it is of society at large. Theological liberalism, like its secular counterparts, has historically been born in the classrooms and nurtured in the journals.

Why is that so? An explanation worth listening to points to at least two significant factors.

The first is that by their very nature, professors and writers are creative folks unwilling to accept the status quo. Always, they're looking for new explanations for things. "Why?" is their constant theme, and existing answers rarely satisfy. And we should be thankful God made some people that way, because in the right context, such a spirit keeps us looking for his truth.

The problem is that we're so often caught up in the wrong context. That's the second reason that academia and the media have a tendency to pull us from right to left. In fact, the first reason—by itself—shouldn't produce any directional tug at all. It would keep us exploring, to be sure, but an openly inquiring mind ought to be as inclined to go north as to go south, to head east as often as it goes west.

What skews the situation is, in fact, the context. Professors and writers, like all of us, have peers. Like all of us, they like to please their peers. The problem is that professors and writers work so exclusively in the world of ideas and values. To please their peers they have to do with those ideas what their peers find satisfactory. That whole process has a tendency to tug the ideas even of well-meaning people in the direction of the peer group.

All this is said not to clobber Christian educators and writers, but to remind them (and the rest of us) what a special responsibility they bear, and what pointed temptations face them along the way in their work. While it is true that all of us are challenged to accept less than biblical standards in our various tasks, it may be that they especially face a relentless call to forsake such a narrow measuring stick in favor of something more popular.

In other words, it's easier for a Christian computer analyst to go to a convention on programming and be accepted by his peers than it is for a Christian biology professor to go to the annual meeting of his professional organization and talk openly about a biblical view of creation. It's easier for a Christian who's an interior designer to win awards from his or her peers than it is for a sociologist who continues to insist that homosexuality is an unacceptable lifestyle.

The pressures are stern. I know that partly because I just participated in the annual convention of the Evangelical Press Association, a gathering of journalists and publishing personnel firmly committed to the authority of Scripture. This year, for professional purposes, we met jointly with people from the Associated Church Press—a much more liberal group with only a sprinkling of evangelically oriented members. Through the three days, I was impressed how often I was tempted to trim my own sails, to refrain from saying what I really believed, just so I could have the respect of those professional colleagues from the other end of the ideological spectrum. They just kept calling me to the middle of the road.

Christians should pray regularly for teachers and writers who live with those pressures. In many respects they are the guardians of what we hold dear. It is important that they be found faithful.

God's Point of View: He Sets the Rules for Any Interviews

BY JOEL BELZ
FEBRUARY 16, 1991

Now that you've got your W-2 form in hand but are feeling increasingly guilty that you haven't gotten around to your tax returns yet (you still have two months to go!), take a fresh look at one of the Bible's most famous passages about taxes—Matthew 22:15-22.

Except I'd like to suggest that when Jesus delivered his short "Render unto Caesar" speech, he had something other than taxes or church-state relations on his mind.

Instead of giving the Pharisees a tax table telling them what proportion of their income they could deduct for charitable giving for the calendar year A.D. 29, Jesus was telling them they had to get their whole worldview straight.

In other words, don't deal with details until you get the big picture in focus. Don't fine-tune until you're on the right channel.

The two main points Jesus was teaching as he flipped the denarius over in his palm were these:

First: Don't pretend to be interested in the fine points of a God-centered worldview if your heart isn't right.

Make no mistake: Jesus' answer to the Pharisees was a put-down. He wasn't really answering their question at all. He knew the phoniness of their hearts, and he wasn't going to give them the satisfaction of an answer so long as they had no intention of listening in the first place.

It's easy for us to be in the same position. We go through the formalities of studying and discussing what a "Christian" position might be on a particular subject—when deep in our hearts we really have no intention of adjusting our lives once we find the answer. We're just intellectualizing. Like the Pharisees, we're often much more interested in proving our own point of view than we are in discovering God's truth on a matter.

When that's our posture, Jesus says he's not interested in providing a response. He holds his wisdom for those who ask with sincerity.

Second: Jesus doesn't offer cheap answers. What the Pharisees desperately wanted was a pocket calculator that would let them figure with certainty how much belonged to Caesar and how much to the temple. Then they could add those calculations to all their other rules and regulations.

What we want today is a handy-dandy floppy disk we can pop into our micro-processors that will crunch all the prophetic references of Daniel and Ezekiel, along with how the price of oil futures affects the plight of the Palestinians. The printout available just fifteen minutes from now will tell us whose side in the Gulf War is more just.

We want quick, quantified answers. We're modern-day Pharisees.

To us, as to the Pharisees, Jesus simply says, "OK, if that's the kind of answer you want, I'll give it. Give to Caesar what is Caesar's, and to God what is God's."

You can almost hear the Pharisees muttering as they wander off, "We don't know any more than we did before we asked! Now we have a whole slew of new questions. No way do we dare go back and ask him how much belongs to Caesar and how much to God. How embarrassing!"

That's the point. If you come with the wrong spirit or seeking simplistic answers, God keeps you in your ignorance.

When you're ready to bow before him and express your willingness to expose yourself patiently to the marvelous complexities of his wisdom, then he answers. That's when he expands your worldview, sending you away with delight instead of frustration.

How Embarrassing! Prayer As Our Last Resort

BY JOEL BELZ
MARCH 2, 1991

Praying in emergencies is certainly a good thing to do.

I had a friend some years ago who, whenever he heard a siren—no matter how distant—insisted that we stop where we were and pray for whoever it was that might be involved. "It's an emergency," he'd always argue, "isn't it? Somebody's in trouble."

Just the same, even with wailing sirens all over the world, there's a right way and a wrong way to go about praying. I think my friend did it right. I'm less certain as I drive down the street and see the plastic signs encouraging me to:

PRAY FOR OUR TROOPS
IN THE MIDDLE EAST

Is this the same society where only a few months ago prayer was more and more often being declared just a marginal and private function? Where we couldn't go more than a few months without appealing some case to a high court to determine when and where prayer was to be allowed and when and where it wasn't?

To turn then and plaster our thoroughfares with calls to pray for the troops is a little cheap. Our nation has become one giant foxhole, with everyone in it suddenly getting religion. We should be ashamed.

But oddly, prayer both is and isn't something you properly do as a matter of last resort.

Clearly, it's right to pray early in a situation. Before things get desperate, and while everything still seems relatively under control, it's a good thing to pour our hearts out to God—maybe with little more than a humble expression of our thanksgiving. The problem is, we humans don't regularly get at it so early in the game.

We wait instead until things get tough, until the sirens go off. It's not just a war in the Middle East that prompts us then to scurry back to God, a little fearful perhaps that we've forgotten where and how to find him. A really bad depression might do it too, or an earthquake like the one in San Francisco seventeen months ago, or maybe an AIDS epidemic much more widely spread than the one we already have. God has his ways of getting our attention, and they tend to drop us to our knees.

Except that far too often, we're only on our knees as a figure of speech. Our hearts are even slower to bend than our legs are.

That's what's wrong with the plastic signs on the roadside telling us to pray for our soldiers. They have a tone of presumption about them, as if it's our right all of a sudden, after long periods of having neglected prayer, suddenly to assume it's our right again. Shouldn't a little period of contrition come in between?

Certainly it should.

Amazingly, God's extraordinary mercy makes itself evident again and again even when we barge undeserving and unprepared into his presence. Still he welcomes us, in the moment of our desperation. The sirens of our lives go off, and because he is who he is, God hears.

Yet how much better to be able to claim those rich promises about approaching God's throne boldly. How much more reassuring to come before him out of a long-established habit rather than in panic. Then you're fully prepared for that situation Hebrews calls a "time of need" (Hebrews 4:16).

If you're going to do that, though, you don't wait around for a reminder from a plastic sign on the side of the road.

No Permanent Enemies

BY MARVIN OLASKY
SEPTEMBER 24, 1994

"God is my judge, not you, Senator Metzenbaum." With those words Clarence Thomas, his cup of anguish filled, turned on the Ohio Democrat who was hounding him during the Anita Hill hearings of 1991.

I heard those words repeatedly during the ensuing weeks. My third-oldest son Daniel then was six, and I had told him that the name "Daniel" means "God is my judge." When he heard Clarence Thomas's statement on the news, he was off and running. "God is my judge, not you, Senator Metzenbaum," Daniel said dozens of times, relishing the rhythm (six one-syllable words, then a ringing six-syllable title and name).

It was sheer poetry, like "Are we there yet?" So you can see—even ignoring for the moment the seventy-seven-year-old senator's lifetime of destructively liberal politics—why I am unlikely to be writing a column offering two cheers for Howard Metzenbaum. And yet, here it is. The reason: Mr. Metzenbaum has shepherded his Multiethnic Placement Act of 1994 through the Senate as part of a larger bill, and a House-Senate conference committee is likely to approve the measure for final passage by both houses.

The Metzenbaum initiative, if passed and enforced, will mean that governmental groups and adoption agencies can no longer keep black kids in foster-care limbo, waiting for black adoptive parents to show up, if there are white parents ready to adopt them. (Now it's not unusual for black children—who make up 40 percent of the 200,000 kids in America available for adoption—to wait up to five years for adoption; some never find families.)

Senator Metzenbaum pushed hard for the act despite the opposition of one of those classic Democratic Party interest groups, the National Association of Black Social Workers, which worries that black kids brought up in white homes may see themselves primarily not in terms of race but as Christians, or Texans, or baseball fans. From the stories adoption advocates tell, Senator Metzenbaum heard a moving story of a child's life ruined and just got fed up. "It outrages me that poor little kids suffer because of the views of some social workers," the *Wall Street Journal* quoted him as saying.

Some other politicians, on this issue, also have had enough. The support of Representative Kweisi Mfume, a Maryland Democrat who heads the Congressional Black Caucus, may make the difference for the measure in the House. "I've caught some grief on this," he said. "But I've seen a lot of kids who have been denied the opportunity to be adopted, and that breaks your heart."

There's a lesson in such comments for Christians who are always looking for the cracked-wide-open heart, the heart of stone so broken that its possessor cries out to God for a new model softened by God's grace and ever-after irrigated by Christ's blood. Our hearts desire the big breakthroughs; but let's not overlook the tiny cracks that are evident in men like Mr. Metzenbaum.

For example, when a libertarian comes to oppose abortion not because she hears the screams of either God or an unborn child, but because her political theory is bothered by the attack on personhood that abortion represents, let's welcome her, work alongside her on the particular issue of abortion, and pray that God will break her heart entirely. She is an enemy on many issues but a friend on one, and she may not be a permanent enemy on any.

When a feminist attacks pornography not because she cares about how it ruins lives and breaks up families but because she sees slime photos as part of a universal male plot to oppress women, let's welcome her and work alongside her. At the least, if a local antipornography coalition is successful, a city will be cleaner; and, as we pray, she may move from enemy to friend.

When an abortionist makes a donation to a crisis pregnancy center, let's accept the money and pray that even though the check probably was written to make a public relations point, a tiny flaw in the abortionist's titanium alloy heart may eventually create a crisis. Abortionists wade in evil, but God is their judge, and he takes no pleasure in drowning them.

One summer, before my son Daniel became a Clarence Thomas fan, we were climbing sand dunes along Lake Michigan. When he reached the top, he looked back over the sparkling lake to the west, looked down over the dark trees to the east, and said very dramatically, "Now I have seen the world from above."

Our natural tendency is to think that enemies are permanent. But the view from above displays sea, sand, and darkness, with people traveling from one to another region, sometimes not even knowing where they are going or why they are walking. Let's strive to be patient and let's pray to be kind, even to Senator Metzenbaum.

Anger: A Little Like Sex

BY JOEL BELZ
OCTOBER 15, 1994

There's a difference between anger and meanness. Christians have a right now and then to be angry. We never have a right to be mean.

The more I've listened to the discussion about the rightness or wrongness of the anger so many Christians feel toward the Clinton administration, the more I think we're confusing the two attitudes. It's time to sort them out.

By my count, the Bible includes nearly 400 specific references to anger and being angry. Amazingly, most of them refer to the anger of God. That would suggest that anger, by itself, is not an evil emotion. You might even go so far as to call it a holy response—provided we learn to exercise it in a Godlike fashion. Perhaps it's even appropriate to see our "anger drive" in something of the same light in which we view our "sex drive"—there's a high and holy use for it, but there's also a wrong use. And like the sex drive, the anger drive is volatile and easily subject to major abuse.

All of which is probably why the apostle Paul gives the Christians at Ephesus this simple advice: "In your anger do not sin" (Ephesians 4:26). Some of God's very best gifts are placed immediately adjacent to some of the greatest opportunities for slipping up. He does that so that when we finally master those most delicate issues of personal relationships—when in fact we develop the mind of Christ within us—the glory that results is just that much greater.

But because we are fallen, it isn't easy. Our hearts and minds are so skewed that we develop a mean streak and call it righteous anger. We revise Paul's advice to say: "In your anger, feel free to sin."

So how do you know when anger has turned to meanness, when truly righteous anger has taken on unrighteous aspects?

Part of the problem is that in our common usage, the word *anger* has a whole handful of synonyms. There is indignation, implying righteous anger aroused by what seems to be unjust, mean, or insulting. There is rage, suggesting a violent outburst in which self-control is lost. There is fury, implying a frenzied response bordering on madness. There is ire, used these days mostly in literary contexts, suggesting deep anger in acts, words, and looks. And there is wrath, implying deep indignation expressing itself in a desire to punish or get revenge. Which of those definitions fits the God of the Bible? All five synonyms but ire are in my Bible, referring to God. But clearly, the ideas behind indignation and wrath are more appropriate than those behind fury and rage, at least as spelled out in the dictionary definitions just cited.

The word *mean* also has some synonyms—but not a single one appropriate as a description of God. "Ignoble, base, small-minded, petty," the dictionary says. "Stingy, miserly, penurious, bad-tempered, vicious, contemptibly selfish, disagreeable, malicious."

So the question comes: When folks worry about the anger of a good many evangelical Christians, are they worrying about something justifiable from the first list or unjustifiable from the second? It's an important question, for it speaks of the difference between holiness and sin.

Right at the center of the whole discussion is the issue of whose interests are at stake. Are we worried about our interests or God's? Is it simply our sense of well-being that has been disturbed, or are we truly jealous for the standards and reputation of God himself?

Those are not necessarily easy questions to answer, for our deceitful hearts trick us even here. But there are some telling questions to ask ourselves.

1. What attribute of God is being offended? Write it down—specifically. God is known by his word and by his works. Which of them is being jeopardized by the thing that has just made you so angry? Spelling it out is a good mental discipline; it makes you more analytical and less emotional.

2. Have you been consistent in applying the standard? If you're upset, for example, that President Clinton has increasingly made it a habit to use the pulpit of some church as a sounding board for his political program, were you just as critical when someone of your own persuasion did the same thing in other settings?

3. Could you sleep on the issue and then feel just as strongly about it? I have a friend who keeps a scrapbook of hot letters he wrote but never sent. It helped him to get the strong feelings out of his system, but he had the good sense, in these cases, to let the sun go down on his wrath precisely so that it would have opportunity to cool. The durability of your anger is not a foolproof test, but it has some legitimacy. Too much of what we do is little more than emotional release.

4. Have you subjected your anger to the counsel of godly people? Pick two or three people known for their good judgment and godly wisdom. Then make it a practice to test your anger by bouncing it off them before you aim it at your enemies. Don't be afraid to choose someone who's bold enough to disagree with you. You—and your arguments—will be sharper for it.

5. Make sure you know your facts. Twice in the last twenty-four hours, I've gotten my dander up over something someone told me—only to discover a few minutes later that there was more to the story. As a journalist, I've discovered that dozens of good stories get ruined by the facts. Such is also too often the case, I fear, with what fuels our anger.

People of The(ir) Word

BY JOEL BELZ
APRIL 1, 1995

Christians, of all people, are people of the word. It's not just that they should be, although that is also the case. But Christians by their essence are people who find their early origins, their present sustenance, and their future promise in an eternal word.

From our very first biblical understanding of things, for example, it was God's powerfully creative word that brought everything we know about into being. Hard as it may be to understand exactly how that remarkable word functioned, it's nonetheless foundational to our whole belief system. God attaches very remarkable significance to the words he utters. So should we.

So central are words for the Christian that in the first chapter of John's gospel we're told flat out, "In the beginning was the Word, and the Word was with God, and the Word was God." The concept of a word is so critical that God is willing to be known, believe it or not, as a word! What possibly is going on?

Many things, including some we certainly don't yet understand. But at least this seems true: Against the rich artwork of all his creation, with all its nuanced ambiguity, there comes a time when God chooses to say, "Now I will speak plainly. Now I will clear up the ambiguity. Now I will use words."

Yes, words can also be ambiguous, and that is part of their beauty. Like all the rest of God's great creation, words—especially in the context of a poetic setting—can have layers of meaning that must be peeled away, little by little, in repeated delight.

But in the end words are different because they have specific, unambiguous meaning. Their ultimate purpose is to help us distinguish, not to muddle, what is being referred to. That's why we have reviews of movies, explications of poems, and critiques of paintings. In the end there's a human longing to use words to explain what it all means. And because words have finally to do with ultimate meaning, words are first and foremost a very biblical and a very Christian concept.

But we live in an age that, in many respects, scorns the importance of words. Image, ambience, atmosphere, context, and tone have all become much more important than mere words. As Marshall McLuhan said a generation ago, "The medium has become the message."

That's why newspaper readership is down and TV watching is up, and why even on TV the evening news ratings are down and the tabloid programs flourish. It's why so many TV and radio commercials are all but wordless, depending instead on mood-setting for their impact. It's why big-screen theaters are doing bigger business than ever, in spite of the fact that you can get the same story line on small screen TVs; a thirty-foot image with crashing sound is simply more compelling than a twenty-one-inch image with only two speakers.

It's also why the Supreme Court looks to the penumbra of the Constitution rather than to its words to discover what is just. It's why several dozen Republican congressmen can sign on to a "Contract with America" that commits them to term limits and six months later walk off as if they had never heard of the concept.

It's why half the people who take marriage vows walk away from them. It's why elementary educators for a generation thought it was more important for little kids to express themselves than it was for them to learn to read. It's why we now have a society where as many as a third of our citizens are functionally illiterate.

It's why, even in evangelical churches, style takes precedence over content, and warm fellowship is a bigger draw than sound teaching.

Words, like dollars, can lose their value.

What an opportunity for people who take words seriously!

If only we did. The tough question for us Christians is whether we in fact live up to our heritage. Or have we too been muted by the culture around us?

Yet even if we have, we can change. Here are a few suggestions of ways you can make yourself more and more a person of the word:

1. Read the Bible more. Way too many of us are pretenders on this one. We say it's important, but our actions don't back us up. Start with Psalm 119 where every single verse is a reminder of how words interact with our daily habits and lives.

2. Take your Bible to church. I'm startled to see how few people carry Bibles anymore. I was even in a four-day Bible study recently where two-thirds of the participants failed to bring Bibles.

3. Keep a dictionary within reaching distance of your dining room

table. At our home in recent months, it's been a rare meal when someone hasn't resorted to an official definition.

4. Look up a new word every day. Stretch yourself into some areas of vocabulary where you're not presently comfortable.

5. Substitute a letter for a phone call in the next twenty-four hours, even if it takes longer and costs thirty-two cents to mail. In today's inter-personal market, phone calls are trite and personal notes are treasured.

6. Remember to keep your word. Think back to the last time you slipped up on a promise, and deliberately go back and make it right.

7. Write a short poem, however dumb, to someone you love.

8. Take notes during the next sermon you hear.

9. For one week, take five minutes every single morning to write a brief thank-you to someone who could use that encouragement.

10. For a second week, keep a 100-word diary every single evening.

11. Keep a prayer journal. Don't just mumble the things you ask and thank God for. Write them down.

The point all the way through, in fact, is that the very process of writing something down makes realists of us. It forces us to come to grips with the typical gap between our good intentions and what we actually accomplish.

With God, there is no such gap. When he says something, it's as good as done. That's why he could speak the worlds into being.

But even God has been gracious to write down his words—and that dependable written record is one of the main differences between what Christians hold to and the flimsy basis of so many other religions. Start celebrating that difference by reminding yourself regularly that you too are a person of the word.

"He Went Too Far—But . . ."

BY JOEL BELZ
MAY 6, 1995

That there is even a hint of justification among evangelical Christians for the spirit of exasperation that led to the Oklahoma City bombing should be an embarrassment to all of us who wear the label of biblical Christianity.

"Well, obviously, he went too far," a Christian friend said to me a couple of days ago about Timothy McVeigh, the first suspect arrested in connection with the bombing. "But I can understand the frustration he felt at what's going on in Washington."

Sympathy of that sort has no place in a biblically instructed worldview. It comes from the same confused perspective that doesn't quite condone the shooting of an abortionist, but still identifies too warmly with the frustration that led to the shooting.

In both cases, at root it's a faithless denial of our confidence in God as we live as his people in a hostile environment.

It's an oddity of the evangelical subculture that we keep attracting to ourselves a small cadre of Rambo-type vigilantes who are certain they have to be God's defenders. They talk tough, they swagger about, and they constantly imply that a clenched fist and the business end of a gun are the ultimate expressions of even God's power.

Domestically, these are the fellows who can recite every reference in the Bible to male headship in marriage, but never mention the parallel instructions for men to love their wives with the same tenderness Christ showed for the church. They've learned the proverb that if you spare the rod, you'll spoil your child, but they never quote Paul when he warns fathers not to be so overbearing that they produce bitterness in their children.

Ecclesiastically, these are the folks who get their doctrinal details right but can't make the same doctrine attractive to anyone. They applaud the apostles when they talk about discipline, but get skeptical if you quote those same apostles about being all things to all people.

In civil life, these are people whose whole political experience has been unblemished with a single compromise of any kind. In fact, they've probably never even been tempted to political compromise for the simple reason they've never carried on a serious political conversation with someone they disagree with.

World, of course, supports the biblical (if politically incorrect) concept of male headship in the home. We believe the Bible clearly requires male leadership in the church. And we're so typically conservative in most of our political views that some of our liberal friends have long since given up on us. Yet it's precisely because we hold these and many other issues to be part of God's plan for his people that we can't afford to let our image get so terribly distorted as is happening right now.

The good thing to know is that God is sovereign; his power is ample to protect himself, his cause, and his people.

The best way to think of the immensity of God's sovereignty is to sit for a bit and imagine how big evil is—and then to remember that he is much bigger yet. Every time big-time evil has come along—the Philistines, the Babylonians and the Assyrians, Nero, Hitler, the Soviet Union—people have gotten fainthearted and wondered whether God really had something this big in mind when he said he would defeat all our foes. Then God demonstrated that yes, he did have pipsqueaks like that in mind.

So now if we think the abortion industry is a monstrosity that must make God weep; if we think it is loathsome for the federal government to put its great weight behind the homosexual lobby; if indeed we think the U.S. government has become so overweening in its intrusion into so much of our lives that it threatens to take the place of God himself as the one we should trust for our well-being—if all those things are so, and they are indeed, what possible biblical warrant do God's people have to believe that our only recourse is through the arm of the flesh?

We should seek transformation through other means.

God gives his people his Word, which he calls a Spirit-sharpened sword, and equips them through it with words of their own to change other people's minds. Most of us know that Word so shallowly and use it so feebly that we've never experienced its power.

God equips us also with prayer, a weapon terribly underused by God's people against his and our enemies. God's people in other emergencies have talked all night with him, they've begged him, they've cajoled him and bargained with him. We set aside a day a year as a Day of Prayer, and even then spend most of our time doing things besides praying.

Great people of the faith have called these exercises "means of grace." By that, they usually mean it's through these exercises that God normally infuses us with his grace. Through them, he shows mercy to his creatures.

But by them too, we become more graceful people. And God knows, his kingdom needs a few more of them right now.

Feed Him or Destroy Him?

BY JOEL BELZ
NOVEMBER 11, 1995

It's hard to read the book of Psalms without running headlong into a question we'd rather ignore: Why all this talk about enemies?

That's not just a casual theme for David and his coauthors. No fewer than ninety-three times during the 150 Psalms do they make reference to the enemy. You might even call it a preoccupation.

Indeed, if the Psalms had been an Israeli periodical with a letters-to-the-editor page, early Jewish subscribers would almost certainly have complained regularly about the unloving and harsh spirit of the writers.

The New Testament includes another three dozen references or so to the subject of enemies. Like the Old, the New Testament typically recognizes an enemy pretty much as the bad guy. But it is admittedly confusing to compare David's prayers that his enemies be destroyed with the apostle Paul's call to feed an enemy who is hungry. It is that unfolding picture of an enemy that gives us pause.

I couldn't help thinking about enemies this past week when a group of witches gathered for a pre-Halloween public celebration on the courthouse plaza less than a mile from the *World* editorial offices. It was a PR event, one of the witches said, to show the public that witches are really pretty good folks after all, and not the broom-riding, spell-casting, black-hooded evil beings we all have in our minds. All they wanted to do was to recite a few incantations (really, that was their own word), weave a web of rope to bind themselves together, and enjoy a little fellowship (that was also their own word).

Were these men and women my enemies? Were they God's enemies?

Just a few days earlier, President Bill Clinton had announced his own explicit support for new legislation that would make it illegal for an employer to decide not to hire a homosexual person. "This is wrong," the president said. "Individuals should not be denied a job on the basis of something that has no relationship to their ability to perform their work." Clinton aide George Stephanopoulos, meanwhile, was telling the National Lesbian and Gay Journalists Association that the presidential announcement was not just a casual development; he boasted that his boss had "brought gay and lesbian issues out of the closet and into the open."

Does blatant behavior like that make President Clinton my enemy? At least so far as that particular action is concerned, is he God's enemy?

Nor are David's enemies in the Psalms always that easy to identify. Was it King Saul and his foot soldiers, prowling about in the dark for a chance to ambush David? Was it troupes of pagan foreigners who wanted to destabilize Israel? Was it the disgruntled loner who, John Hinckley-style, wanted a place in history by assassinating the king?

Or, to put a loftier spin on things, were David's enemies those people who couldn't abide the fact that David was a man after God's own heart, and whose opposition to David was really opposition to God himself? In short, was David's grumbling about his enemies the kind of simple human fearfulness everybody faces at one time or another—or was it rooted in a high and holy loyalty to his Lord?

Those are questions serious Christians should ask when they debate either each other or non-Christians in the volatile climate of public policy issues. If the Bible itself is ambiguous about who David's enemies were, we shouldn't be surprised if a similar ambiguity surrounds our own efforts to categorize people we aren't quite sure are enemies or allies.

The wimpish way out is to pretend that there are no enemies at all. The Bible, of course, is never so naive. It always assumes there are evil people who want to destroy good people, that there are serious God-haters intent on profaning all that is holy. A biblically mature outlook is one that assumes the active opposition of the enemy—indeed, the opposition of an enemy "who prowls around like a roaring lion looking for someone to devour" (1 Peter 5:8).

Yet after making that assumption, the biblically mature person is one who first exercises great care in identifying who that enemy is, and then determines with cautious wisdom whether the circumstances call for feeding him or wiping him out.

And we make those choices against the backdrop of the knowledge that we too—all of us—were once God's enemies. God, you see, has always exercised a mysterious choice with reference to those who oppose him. Some of them, he has destroyed. And some of them, through a process we can only marvel at, he has made into people he now calls friends.

Health and Welfare

Hearts, Knees, and Health Care

BY JOEL BELZ
DECEMBER 21, 1991

I think my mother and my father-in-law have a great deal to do with our national health care crisis.

In a sense, I'm reluctant to talk about personal issues in a public way. Yet that very reluctance contributes to the problems we face.

Briefly, I'm not sure we Americans can afford the health care we all think we deserve. Most of us, I think, have such doubts.

But when it comes to someone we love very much, like I do my mother and my father-in-law, we tend to set aside the knowledge that we can't afford what we then go right ahead and do.

Nearly two years ago, after trying to keep up with my hard-working mother for seven decades, her heart said it couldn't do that anymore. Mother was hurried to a good hospital where the best of medicines and techniques were used to reconstruct what had gone wrong. Without such care she would almost certainly have died or spent the rest of her years as an invalid.

Then last month my father-in-law's knee, after flexing flawlessly several million times while he split wood and hunted deer for sixty-nine years, said it would do so in the future only by inflicting great pain. A pain-free metal alloy replacement was available, however, and Dad Jackson had it installed a few days after Thanksgiving. The doctors tell him it's probably good for as long as he is.

A heart, a knee—and medical bills of at least $50,000. We talk about the heart and the knee, but we discreetly avoid discussing the bills, because they are for people we love. And we're given the luxury of avoiding those discussions because another family member, Uncle Sam, has said he'll take care of most medical costs for older people—at least for the time being.

So that you don't worry about invasion of privacy, both my mother and my father-in-law have said it's OK to write openly about them here. They've said that because they're concerned citizens who understand they've benefited from a generous society that too often pretends it can pay for luxuries it can't in fact afford.

By quietly passing big bills on to invisible bill-payers, we obscure two important issues that we ought to be discussing:

1. What is a "luxury" when it comes to medical care? Does God give all his people a "right" to the best? Or does he intend that while some people get Cadillac hearts, others will have to do with fuel pumps from Volkswagen Beetles? What about spending $150,000 to preserve the life of a premature baby, or $100,000 to extend the life of someone who is certain to die soon anyway? Just being pro-life doesn't pay those bills. Our tendency is to think when it's someone else they should be willing to get by, but when it's us or our family only the best will do. How do we defend such a tendency biblically? Is that just an extension of the way we've all been shaped by our materialistic age?

2. What can we really afford? Because we're reluctant to talk about such issues, and because the bills have mostly been paid up until now, we never get down to discussing what we could afford if the present system weren't in place.

For instance, my mother's heart and my father-in-law's knee produced some big bills—but nothing that their twelve children and some prudent planning couldn't have handled if push had come to shove. But what if there weren't twelve children? Or what if there were, but they were all unemployed or had minimum-wage jobs? Is there ever a place in health care simply to say, "Sorry, Mom. Sorry, Dad. We'd like that for you, but we just can't afford it"?

Our present system may do us a favor in one sense by sparing us such considerations. But the favor is short-lived if by ignoring the discussion we actually only delay it. If we assume the bills are being paid when in fact they're not, even our parents will agree we're not being kind or faithful to our children.

Because God's providence is so much involved in such discussion, Christians ought to be leading the way in pursuing the answers our whole society needs.

Welfare God's Way

BY JOEL BELZ
OCTOBER 16, 1993

As the welfare debate heats up anew, as every headline for the last week suggests that it already has, biblically-minded Christians need to sharpen their thinking on the subject. Too much of what many of us tend to say about welfare is little more than a tired conservative rehash of ideas—however true—that have failed for several generations now to persuade skeptical liberals. Wouldn't it be better if this time around we specifically grounded our arguments more forcefully in God's own words?

For as big a failure as the liberal welfare programs have been for the last thirty years—and the failure has been colossal—those of us who have opposed such programs also have to admit that we are usually better at theorizing than we are at demonstrating biblical models of what ought to be done. So long as our models are still abstract instead of concrete, we have little reason to be taken seriously. Worse yet, if the models of Christians cannot be specifically grounded in biblical principle, why should we even bother investing the human and financial resources needed to test them in real life?

It's partly for such reasons that *World* has placed a priority in recent months on stories about Christians involved in flesh-and-blood efforts to establish biblically-based, nongovernmental welfare programs for the needy. We expect to continue highlighting such efforts throughout the United States and around the world as they are called to our attention and as we are persuaded those efforts have validity.

Yet as we do so, it's important that *World* as the teller of those stories and you as the reader exercise diligence to sort out the distinctives of those efforts that are indeed biblically rooted. A Christian worldview says that welfare is just like theology or philosophy or anything else we are serious about; we don't make it up as we go along, but instead look to the Bible for the undergirding principles on which we then build the superstructure.

Are there indeed such principles to guide us in the welfare task? Without pretending to have them all, let me suggest three for starters that have deep biblical roots and enormous potential for revolutionizing the weary welfare debate as it has been carried on so unproductively for so many years between conservatives and liberals.

1. Wealth can be created. This concept, permeating all of Scripture, is intrinsic to God's created order—and it has radical implications for our view of economics and economic restoration. For if wealth cannot be created, then it must be taken from someone or somewhere else. But if it can be created, then the wealth that is already there can be left in place.

The assumption of the welfare state, as most of us have seen it, denies this basic principle. It assumes instead that the only source of wealth for the poor is to take it from those who already have it. And in making that assumption, it flies directly in the face of God's incredibly generous and ingenious order of things.

On the face of the Genesis record, Adam and Eve were not born wealthy people. But right at their disposal God placed the means of discovering all the wealth they could imagine. The natural resources and the wisdom to develop them were God's great gifts to human beings from the first day they woke up in his garden. Those same gifts, however impaired by the fall, are there today for every descendant human being, if we'll only wake up to them.

A few hundred years later, God didn't call the people of Israel simply to inherit fully accomplished wealth in the Promised Land of Canaan. Instead, the territory was to be developed, subdued, and expanded by God's trusting and confident children.

The same picture confronts us in the New Testament. Paul tells God's people to work with their hands so they don't have to be a drag on others—and to create some wealth to give to those who really need it.

The Bible is replete with this crucial and upbeat idea. It is foundational to a discussion of welfare, and we Christians should be in the vanguard of those teaching the principle. In a discouraging setting, it offers a glimmer of hope.

2. Work is essential. Here's a principle we don't have to infer by com-

paring six passages of Scripture; Paul says it flat out: "If a man will not work, he shall not eat" (2 Thessalonians 3:10).

Yes, there may come a few blurry situations (see point 3 below). But the standard is set about as clearly as anyone could set it. Under President Clinton's welfare reform a few months ago, it was two years and out. Under the new Republican proposals, it may be more like two months and out. Either way, stating it that briefly misses the point.

Work isn't meant to be punitive but productive. We don't make the lazy person get a job as a penalty for his laziness, but so he can begin to enjoy the fruits of his labor. God's promise is that it's possible to create wealth. He wants all his people to eat the fruit of that promise.

So Christians need to do more than sit back grumpily and tell people to get jobs. They need instead to help find such jobs for those who don't have them, assist with job training, and help those with entry-level jobs move up the ladder as swiftly as they can. All this is part of taking God at his word.

3. Help must be personal. This knife cuts both ways. For if the solutions to our society's horrible welfare needs are not to be found institutionally in the federal or state governments, neither are they likely to be found institutionally elsewhere—even in the church and its various agencies. Assistance of the kind that really helps will be personal.

That may be too costly a message for most of us who are Christians, but we need to hear it and then to practice it. The model in recent years of Christian couples taking unwed mothers into their homes for counsel, nurture, and personal care is one perhaps we need to apply now to a variety of other situations. Instead of rushing to reestablish orphanages, can we find enough Christian homes to take in the hundreds of thousands of youngsters who need them? Can we take in the unemployed for several weeks at a time? However difficult those assignments might be, they are probably easy compared to personally taking in the homeless.

Yet the model of the Bible is almost always one of sacrificial, personal involvement rather than arm's-length, detached institutional help. (The story of the Good Samaritan leans heavily toward the personal, then allows a bit for the institutional.) Not the least of the advantages is that up-close involvement provides up-close accountability. Is this fellow a good guy who just needs some temporary help, or is he a freeloader? If he's in your house, you'll know.

Who can deny that in his greatest welfare act of all time, God became

intensely personal? No committee, no relief agency, no congressional bill
seemed appropriate to deal with our waywardness and slovenly ways. We
all needed personal attention, and that's what we got from his own Son.

The next time you say you want the government out of welfare, think
too about all the implications—and whether you're ready to put your life
where your mouth is.

Re-asking Cain's Question

BY MARVIN OLASKY
OCTOBER 22, 1994

In California, Texas, Florida, and other states, welfare reform is becoming a key campaign issue. Sound bites—"two years and out!"—are flying.
The welfare structure is so corrupt that the temptation to play Lizzie
Borden politics with it—"Lizzie Borden took an ax and gave the system
forty whacks"—is hard to resist.

If Republicans win big next month, they will have the brawn to swing
the ax; Bill Clinton, unless he is willing to alienate his liberal core, will
keep pushing the cosmetic changes he already has proposed; the result will
be either nothing or a compromise that leaves everyone frustrated. Next
year, then, will be an opportune time to propose a radical Christian alternative, one that will not win immediate acceptance but could have legs—
if some young Republican congressmen lead the way toward a new,
church- and community-based, effective antipoverty system.

Since a book I wrote on poverty-fighting, *The Tragedy of American
Compassion*, has been getting some attention lately, I had dinner in
Washington recently with three congressmen who are involved with welfare reform. All three are professing Christians; all three have their hearts
in the right place; all three were asking the right question: "What biblical
principles should be brought to bear on welfare reform?"

That led us into conversation about the religious underpinnings of our
current system. In essence, theological universalists early in this century
argued that "If anyone goes to hell, then God is unfair." Later in this century, when the federal government became our new god, advocates of what

I call *social universalism* began to say, "If anyone is poor, then Government is unfair." Welfare became an entitlement.

These days orthodox Democrats make up the social universalist regiments; neo-orthodox Democrats sometimes talk about work requirements for welfare, but their restrictions are easily avoided because they can't escape the social universalistic faith. The Republican response, however, is often *social darwinism*: Just as Darwin's theory argued that progress comes only by a survival of the fittest, so social darwinists propose that the poor should be left to their own resorts. (Most, as they die off, will eliminate a barrier to the evolutionary progress of humanity.)

There is an alternative to both social universalism and social darwinism; historically in American culture, it was what could be called *social calvinism*. Just as Calvinists preached (and preach) the Gospel to everyone, not knowing who in God's providence will respond, but aware that some will and some will not, for reasons we do not understand, so social calvinists up to a century ago fought poverty effectively by offering spiritual challenge and entry-level jobs to the poor.

In the nineteenth century, the poor who responded to social calvinist appeals began moving out of poverty. The climb was hard, but Christians were there to help. To the able-bodied who did not respond, the apostle Paul's doctrine was applied: "If a man will not work, he shall not eat." But as universalism pushed back Calvinism theologically early in this century, so social universalism became the soil for new governmental programs from the 1930s through the 1960s—and the rest is misery.

Christian members of Congress should accept neither liberal stinginess (continuation of a social universalistic governmental system that supposedly relieves us of the obligation to exercise personal compassion toward those in need) nor conservative stinginess (substitution of a social darwinist system that is cheaper but even colder). The critical task in welfare reform over the next few years is to eliminate government's failed programs *and* to have something to put in their place: a Bible-based system of charity and challenge that can activate groups within churches to work intensively with welfare recipients who need more than a check.

Since many churches have emphasized development of small groups during the 1990s, the infrastructure for such a program already is in place. But the small groups must be motivated to look outward by bringing into the midst of each a needy person or family. Pastors will be key motivators here; they should explain that social universalists want to be their brothers' keepers (remember, it was Cain, not God, who phrased the question that way), and social darwinists are sometimes their brothers' killers, but those who follow in Christ's steps are their brothers' helpers.

We can't keep those who insist on ruining their souls and bodies from doing so, but we should not cooperate in the killing either; we should help them by offering both the Gospel and material opportunity. Small groups can do both in a way that governmental bureaucrats cannot, and legislators can help by defunding the bureaucracy and using money budgeted for welfare to offer tax credits that will compensate church "compassion circles" for their out-of-pocket material support of the person in need. In that way, people of all income brackets will have more opportunity to become their brothers' helpers.

There's much more to this plan, but it will only get moving if tough-headed, warmhearted leaders commit themselves to planting a tree every time they swing an ax.

The Word and the Grub

BY MARVIN OLASKY
NOVEMBER 19, 1994

"Hide it under a bushel, No!" In celebration of the Thanksgiving season, I have on my office door at the University of Texas a cartoon depicting two Pilgrims sitting across from two Indians, and one of the Indians is saying, "Rumor has it you're from the religious right."

That cartoon works on several levels. First, it is (I have to admit it) an in-your-face reminder to hostile colleagues who think that Christians who gain a place at a state university should be thankful enough to be silent about God. But the cartoon also reminds me of how much pinkskins and redskins had to give to each other: Friendly natives showed needy settlers how to grow food for the body, and Christians among the European immigrants offered food for the soul. They did not merely go along to get along.

Biblical interaction between homeless individuals and volunteers who are better off in body and soul also aids both sets of individuals—if done properly. Men and women in the gutter learn to step heavenwards, and the helpers not only feel God's pleasure in giving but witness with their own eyes the changes. Guests at the Chicago Hilton who suddenly have their hearts transmuted by God generally do not alter their outward appearance; but two blocks away, at the Pacific Garden Mission, men who used to sit in vomit-soaked stupor dress cleanly and sing hymns.

Good homeless shelters offer challenge and produce changed lives. At many shelters this month, however, aid to the homeless has lost its biblical saltiness and is giving way to a thankless Thanksgiving feast of giblets mixed with gimme's and grunts. Liberal homeless programs from sea to shining sea have become enablers of drug addiction and alcoholism and produced only a cross-class backlash against the enablers. Wealthy residents of northwest Washington, D.C., and low-income residents of central San Diego are among the multitudes who have spent 1994 fighting the establishment or expansion of homeless feeding programs in their neighborhoods.

The San Diego war has become so heated that its theological disputes are animating even the pages of the *Los Angeles Times*. On one side stands Roman Catholic Msgr. Joseph Carroll, head of the massive St. Vincent de Paul Village for the Homeless. The Village sleeps 850 people, feeds another 600 to 800 who sleep on downtown streets, employs 270 men and women, and has a budget of $20 million. On the other side is City Council member Juan Vargas, who represents blue-collar neighborhoods adjacent to the shelter.

The *Times* quoted "Father Joe" Carroll (who has been lauded by the United Nations and the Bush and Clinton administrations) as saying, "There were 5,000 people with nothing to eat and Christ fed them, and he didn't require drug testing. Was he being an enabler?" Reporter Tony Perry then quoted Mr. Vargas: "If someone was on drugs or alcohol and killing themselves or others, I don't think Christ would say, 'That's interesting, now here's some free food.' He would say, 'Wait a minute, you have a sin . . . I'm not going to let you continue in your addiction.'"

Layman Vargas is right. A "rub-a-dub-dub, pass out the grub" ethos does not provide the true food that the truly hungry need. In the Gospels, as throughout the Bible, the Word always preceded the grub. Jesus had the power to feed all, but he fed the hungry only twice—and both experiences came after crowds were stranded without food because they had listened to him for a long time. Even so, word apparently spread that the Word brought grub; once expectations were raised, Jesus practiced his church shrinkage strategy by giving a withering "I am the bread of life" sermon.

Since the universalistic homeless feeding programs of the religious left are not Christian, my sympathies are with Mr. Vargas and the poor persons who have worked hard to create decent living spaces for their children. It's important that barely-hanging-on poor communities not be pushed over the edge. "If we keep doing what we're doing, we're only going to create a homeless ghetto," Mr. Vargas says. And yet, if neighborhoods can keep religious organizations from serving the poor, then such activities become a privilege rather than a right, and even biblical charities may lose legal protections.

There is no easy answer here. The overall lesson is that theology is destiny. Once programs offered in the name of Christ become unbiblical enablers of destruction, we are confronted with bad choices. Christians in San Diego, Washington, and other cities can support restrictions on the expansion of homeless shelters that enable consumption of drugs and alcohol, but they should exercise great discernment to keep bad charity, once again, from driving out the good.

The lesson for all of us at Thanksgiving time, and all through the year, is to stay on the narrow path that Christ outlines for us; once we enter the broad California freeway, we're in trouble. The *Los Angles Times* quoted San Diego Mayor Susan Golding as saying about the homelessness impasse, "The last thing we ought to do is make this a theological discussion." No, that's the first thing.

Ledges, Not Ledgers

BY MARVIN OLASKY
JANUARY 14, 1995

When my son David and I were playing a battle simulation board game called Gettysburg late last year, each of us was careful to avoid a headlong assault on the other's fortified positions. Flank attacks—maneuvering troops to gain a temporary preponderance of forces at the end of the opponent's line—were essential to success in the War Between the States, and they are also emerging as a tactic in the welfare reform struggle that has just begun.

Last month Democrats who had been on the defensive since the November rout probed the weak side of the Republican formation and drew first blood. Realizing that their best shot is to portray the GOP as the party of Scrooge, Democrats (styling themselves no longer as Friends of Bill but as Friends of Oliver Twist) slammed into the Orphanage Patrol at the end of the Republican line and sent it scurrying for cover. Even when liberal magazines sent reporters to new model orphanages and discovered that Dickens is dead, they counted the cost of such homes and concluded that Republicans have not only loose lips but rusty calculators.

Republican leaders, not wanting to fight a battle on ground the Democrats choose, are now setting up new defensive lines. In one respect this is fine, because an emphasis on orphanages makes people forget that welfare reform is the latest battle in the War for the Family, and that the biblical goal for that war should be to have a child brought up by a father and a mother, not by public officials (that is the road away from true compassion), nor by two "fathers" or two "mothers" (that is the path to perversion), nor by one parent—although there are some times within God's providence when that is unavoidable.

If we keep that understanding in mind, then orphanages should be seventh on the agenda, not first, in any discussion of how to contain the social disaster that a sharp rise in illegitimacy is creating. Think of it this way: Any society that allows, encourages, and even enables sexual activity outside of marriage is placing its young people on a slippery slope. Imagine, as millions are sliding down, that there are seven ledges on which they may come to rest. The first ledge, a safe perch, is abstinence until marriage, so that a child once conceived starts out with the care of a father and a mother. When people slide by that ledge, here comes a second: Public policy and private aid should encourage marriage before or shortly after birth, so that the born child starts out with two parents. When the slide continues so that a baby is born and the potential marriage is stillborn, adoption is the best alternative, so that a child gains two parents.

Only when the slide continues and single parenthood is inevitable do other ledges come into sight. The fourth ledge is an extended family, so that a child who is missing a parent has contact with grandparents, aunts, and uncles. The fifth ledge is made up of big brother and big sister programs, so that a child without sufficient family gains some volunteer support and challenge. The sixth ledge is made up of aid to the mother, so she does not have to bear the entire burden alone. (Historically, church and private aid programs that offer compassionate challenge to recipients have worked best.)

Seventh, and only seventh, in that sequence of ledges—far down the slope—comes the orphanage. That we have to think about orphanages at all shows how slippery and vast the slope has become during the past three decades, and how small in comparison the ledges. (Particularly the adoption ledge: There are adoptive homes for babies and toddlers of all races, but not for children seven or older who have been abused for years; if two-year-olds whose mothers could not care for them were given adoptive homes rather than five years of trauma in revolving-door temporary shelters, the need for orphanages would be slight.) Rather than race to build orphanages, the emphasis should be on repairing the six ledges higher up.

Some Republicans are ready to go to work on the repair job, but others fear talk of family values and want to do their own flank attack by turning welfare into a ledger book question: "We're not talking about values, just about money." Will the orphanage skirmish, incidental though it was, frighten some Republicans into backing off from analysis of family structure? If so, then liberal Democrats will have won, even if they have to swallow some cuts in welfare expenditures. Republicans need to emphasize not the ledger but the ledges of real welfare reform.

Fear or Faith?

BY M A R V I N   O L A S K Y
M A R C H   1 1 ,   1 9 9 5

When children are about ready to go off to college, a father's mind starts flashing back to early days. When my oldest son Pete was little and my wife, Susan, was volunteering at the crisis pregnancy center, Pete and I used to walk around and play "the four things game," in which he was supposed to tell me the essential difference between three items and one other item. For example, I would point out to him a number on a house, a dog, a trash can, and a baby in a stroller and then ask, "Which is different?" Such a question, of course, can be sliced and diced in lots of different ways through multi-perspectival analysis, but Pete gave the answer that warms a daddy's heart: "Baby—'cause he's a person."

"The four things game" was early SAT preparation, I suppose, or maybe basic pro-life training. But what's depressing these days is that some pro-life groups with good intentions are nevertheless messing up in "the four things game." Faced with a governmental welfare system that treats poor women and babies as numbers, or as animals to be fed and petted, and eventually as trash to be discarded, some pro-lifers don't see that persons deserve better: they defend the present system, fearing that a cap on welfare cash benefits will lead to more abortions.

Such a defense is difficult, since the current welfare system's undermining of work, family, and many other gifts of God is widely understood to be wrong. "Two wrongs don't make a right" is the common sense/common grace counter to the notion of fighting the evil of abortion by embracing the evil of governmental welfare. Such an answer, however, is not going to satisfy pro-lifers who argue that welfare is the lesser of two evils and thus justifiable. To answer the single-issue opponents of abortion (and there is no better issue to be single-issue about), we need to ask whether the current welfare system really does result in fewer abortions than would otherwise take place.

I've been noting over the last five years that the recent expansion of abortion and welfare has a common basis: the culture of irresponsibility that emerged during the 1960s and took root during the 1970s. The parallel burgeoning of these two modern curses suggests a parallel cure: the recovery of responsibility, for which we probably need revival and reformation. As *National Review* recently argued (and I cannot say it better, so here comes an extended quotation), "The overall effect of [welfare] cash benefits is to increase the number of abortions by removing an economic disincentive to conception. The more pregnancies out of wedlock, the more abortions there will be—now and in the future. Girls born to single mothers, for instance, are twice as likely to engage in early sexual activity and thus to be candidates for abortion."

National Review pointed out that the economic arguments of pro-lifers opposed to welfare reform would have bizarre effects if applied generally. For example, we would have to fight "any attempt to hold 'deadbeat dads' responsible for their children (since they would then pressure expectant mothers to have abortions). In general, these arguments abandon any attempt to restore personal moral responsibility, replacing it with short-term financial incentives. But that is exactly the mixture that has produced the present epidemic of illegitimacy and abortion. Why embrace it now?"

Let's play an adult version of "the four things game." Who is different— a persevering missionary, a U.S. marine, a conscientious crisis pregnancy center counselor, or Dr. Zarkov of the 1930s Flash Gordon movies? The answer is Dr. Zarkov, who boasts of his travel on "a rocket ship of my own design." The other three all realize that we travel on a ship of someone else's design and should obey that superior authority. For the missionary and the counselor, the commander is in heaven and not on earth, but all three can have in common the marine slogan, *Semper fidelis*—always faithful.

Christians who care about both unborn and born persons need to be faithful to biblical teaching. If we pray, "Always successful," we arrogantly intrude on God's sovereign prerogatives. But if we hope to be always *faithful*, we cast our eyes on God, the object of our faith, who tells us not to do evil in the hope that good may come.

Our goal should be not just welfare reform, and not welfare elimination, but welfare replacement through development of a new system based on churches, private charities, and a culture of responsibility. "Be all you can be" is the marines' fine recruiting line. The first step toward moving in that direction for welfare recipients is to replace the current system so they can be more than numbers or pets.

What the Poor Need

BY MARVIN OLASKY
MARCH 25, 1995

Three decades ago, the Protestant debates concerning welfare essentially pitted theological liberals against evangelicals. In one corner stood the National Council of Churches, which—in a great reversal from church positions of the nineteenth century—argued that government can and should conquer poverty by passing out material aid to every poor person. In the other corner stood evangelical magazines such as *Christianity Today*, which observed that "Faith in God puts courage, compassion, and determination into the hearts of men. These are the qualities that conquer poverty and solve other social problems."

Today evangelicals are not united on the need to fight poverty primarily through Christ's grace rather than Caesar's gifts. Some even quote Jesus' statement, "I was hungry and you gave me something to eat, I was thirsty and you gave me something to drink . . ." to argue against attempts to restructure welfare. Liberal use of the Matthew 25 quotation and others, though, raises severe questions of biblical interpretation.

Is the Bible divided against itself? The Old Testament emphasizes not alms but opportunities to glean, and not subsidies for sluggards but exhortations to be industrious. Was Jesus telling us to forget all that?

Is Jesus divided against Paul? The apostle provided to the Thessalonians and us not a suggestion but a rule: "In the name of the Lord Jesus Christ, we command you, brothers, to keep away from every brother who is idle. . . . 'If a man will not work, he shall not eat'" (2 Thessalonians 3:6, 10).

Is Jesus divided against himself? He could have turned stones into bread to feed all the hungry people in Israel, but instead he fed only those who came to hear him. And he didn't feed them that quickly either. In Matthew 15 Jesus feeds 4,000 men, along with women and children, only after they were with him, gaining spiritual nourishment, for three days.

Since Scripture is not against Scripture, and since we are told frequently that God is compassionate, we need to understand what biblical compassion means if we are to follow obediently in Christ's steps and not make tracks of our own. Compassion in the Bible is connected to repentance and deliverance. Note Nehemiah 9: "When they were oppressed they cried out to you. From heaven you heard them, and in your great compassion you gave them deliverers." Crying out is essential. As Psalm 103 notes, "The LORD has compassion on those who fear him."

About eighty other biblical verses explain God's definition of compassion, and chapter after chapter help us to understand Jesus' command to give food to the hungry and drink to the thirsty. We are told repeatedly that Jesus is the bread of life and the living water. We should not spiritualize away real material needs, but we should also not deny Christ by giving needy people only physical sustenance.

A generation ago the powerful, mainline denominations and their allies (Quakers were particularly known for liberalism) supported the growth of the welfare state. Their members dominated the big philanthropic organizations, and one ditty summarized well the religious influence at the Ford Foundation: "Take a dozen Quakers, be sure they're sweet and pink / Add one discussion program, to make the people think; / Brown a liberal education, in television grease / And roll in economics, seasoned well with peace; / Garnish with compassion, just a touch will do / And serve in deep humility, your philanthropic stew."

In 1962 the National Association of Evangelicals' magazine, *United Evangelical Action*, firmly opposed the welfare state and saw dire consequences if worship of governmental Mammon increased: "In striving for total economic security for all men as the supreme goal, the churches may get something like the desired results through the help of friends, agencies, and the patronage of the state, only to discover that one day they are more in debt to them than to Christ, and have lost not only their momentum, but also their unique reason for being in existence."

That is certainly what has happened to mainline churches, now more appropriately labeled oldline or sideline. Here is how Jesus' words, in light of his own teaching and the whole counsel of God, could be modernized for application to welfare statists: "I despaired and you gave me stew, when what I truly needed was my birthright. I was an alcoholic and you gave me money that I used to buy another bottle, while you walked away applauding yourself. I lived for immediate gratification and needed the discipline of work and family, but you gave me shelter without responsibility so that I did not have to look back or ahead. Now depart from me into the eternal fire."

In the evangelical churches, we need to be careful to avoid the same pit.

The Liberal Bible

BY MARVIN OLASKY
SEPTEMBER 30, 1995

As Congress meanders toward significant welfare reform, some members of the religious left pray that President Clinton is readying his veto pen. Their problem, though, is that many of the Bible's warmhearted but hardheaded passages advocate tough love rather than entitlement, so liberals are hard pressed to find scriptural justification for welfare as we know it.

A dab of rewriting here and there could eliminate the bottleneck and provide powerful new rationales for beleaguered social services. Here are humble suggestions for redoing parts of the two books of the Bible written by Luke.

THE PRODIGAL PANHANDLER—*Luke 15*

There was a man who had two sons. The younger one set off for a distant country and there squandered his wealth in wild living. After he had spent everything, he was in need and took a job feeding pigs.

The job was miserable, and the younger son visualized an alternative: "I will go back to my father and say to him, 'Father, I have sinned against heaven and against you.'" He got up and started back toward his father. But while the prodigal son was still a long way off, an official from Beds for the Homeless saw him and convinced him to spend the night.

The shelter offered free food, housing, clothing, and medicine and did not require any work in return. One day turned into a week, and a week into a month, as the prodigal son became used to panhandling in the morning, drinking fortified wine and smoking some joints in the afternoon, and watching movies at the shelter in the evening.

Meanwhile, the father sat on his porch in the late afternoon, hoping to see the prodigal son trudging home. Day after day the father visualized the opportunity to hug him and prepare a feast, but the son never came.

HOW THE GOOD SAMARITAN ACT WAS PASSED—*Luke 10*

A man was going down from Jerusalem to Jericho when he fell into the hands of robbers. They stripped him of his clothes, beat him, and went away, leaving him half dead. A priest happened to be going down the same road, and when he saw the man, he passed by on the other side.

Then a Samaritan, as he traveled, came to where the man was; and when he saw him, he was outraged that some people were so poor that they were forced to steal clothes. He returned to Jerusalem and, using rhetorical brilliance to overcome prejudice against his ethnic group, convinced the Sanhedrin to pass the Good Samaritan Act.

The Act used temple funds to establish Midnight Shepherding Leagues for disadvantaged youths who might otherwise turn to crime along the Jerusalem-Jericho highway. The Act also erected a monument at the spot where the robbery victim had died.

JESUS FOOD STAMPS THE 5,000—*Luke 9*

Jesus taught the crowds all day. As evening approached, the disciples came to him and said, "Because of budget cuts, there isn't enough food. We have here only five loaves of bread and two fish."

Jesus said, "Bring them here to me." And he directed the people to sit down on the grass. Taking the five loaves and the two fish and looking up toward Jerusalem, the capital, he gave thanks and broke the loaves into many pieces.

Each person received a piece redeemable in a local market that had arranged to be reimbursed from the temple treasury. The number of those who ate was about 5,000 men, besides women and children.

ORIGINS OF THE TEMPLE
LUNCH PROGRAM (ACTS 3)

One day Peter and John were going up to the temple. Now a man crippled from birth was being carried to the temple gate, where he was put every day to beg from those going into the temple courts.

When he saw Peter and John about to enter, he asked them for money. But Peter said, "Silver or gold have I none, but what I have I give to you. In the name of Jesus Christ of Nazareth, here is a sandwich."

Taking the food by the right hand, the man ate it quickly and said, "That is the best sandwich I have ever had." Then Peter and John carried him into the temple courts, and he praised the sandwich in a loud voice.

From then on temple authorities passed out sandwiches to all who begged at their gates, and the numbers of such needy persons increased daily.

But What About the Children?

BY MARVIN OLASKY
DECEMBER 23, 1995

But what about the children?

That's the question liberal defenders of the status quo throw at Christians and conservatives who have worked this year to change the current welfare system. But that question can only be dealt with responsibly when two other questions are answered first.

First: Will the changes lead to children being deprived of food, shelter, clothing, or medicine? Answer: Only if welfare administrators refuse to tighten their belts. Only one-quarter of welfare funds now appropriated get to the poor people they are designed to help; much of the rest goes to support federal and state bureaucracies and their political allies in the non-profit sector. If the welfare system were a private corporation, its middle management corps already would have been substantially downsized; as it is, the change needs to be imposed.

Second: Will the changes lead to an improved war against the real enemy, fatalism? Answer: Yes. If poverty itself led to illegitimacy, crime, laziness, and stupidity, the United States could never have become a rich country, because it was poor people—worse off materially than poor individuals today—who built America. But poor children in the past generally had parents who showed by word and deed the virtue of striving to meet challenges. Today many poor children see all around them the apathy of life on welfare—and it's the fatalism that hurts. If welfare reforms help to develop more hard-working, family-honoring parents, their children will be immensely helped.

Welfare hurts children. That's more than a theory. One recent study looked at the earnings of adult men who had grown up poor. The study compared adults of the same race who as children had the same family income, family structure, and parental educational background; the only difference was whether families derived the bulk of income from welfare or work. The study showed that the more welfare income a boy's family had received as he was growing up, the lower his earnings as an adult; but more non-welfare income led to higher adult earning. The bottom line was that hard-working parents, even (and sometimes especially) if poor, generally produce hard-working children.

Sound Christian programs help children. That's also more than a theory. Groups provide assistance at every age from conception through adulthood.

Some 3,000 crisis pregnancy centers throughout the United States offer material, psychological, and spiritual help to young women who are pregnant and do not want to be, and thus help their children to avoid death before birth and gain a better life after they are born. The largest single network of independent local programs, CareNet, has headquarters in Sterling, Virginia.

Bethany Christian Services cuts through the adoption bureaucracy as well as anyone and also is willing to do transracial adoptions at a time when some organizations still look at the skin color rather than the character of potential adoptive parents. About half of the states have Bethany organizations; national headquarters are in Grand Rapids, Michigan.

KidsHope, based in Spring Lake, Michigan, but now expanding nationwide, leads members of congregations to become tutors and mentors of children in poor communities. Children receive significant help, and church members learn to reach out successfully.

Boys Town, based in Omaha but now expanded to several states, has a series of programs for children and families in crisis; family-style homes for abandoned and abused children are the most intensive. Boys Town's proven system gives people with ordinary parenting skills the ability to handle troubled kids.

Teen Challenge, headquartered in Springfield, Missouri, has over 140 local chapters devoted to helping young people escape addiction or alcoholism. Teen Challenge leaders, generally ex-addicts themselves, understand that people do drugs or get drunk daily because they have holes in their souls that only God can fill.

But what about the children? Two thousand years ago Jesus Christ came into the world to suffer with us (that is the literal meaning of *compassion*) and to die for us. In this year of our Lord 1995, it is a great blessing to see Christians who follow in his steps. And it is a great mistake to be panicked into supporting programs that present "buy one, get one" offers: Here's bread, but along with it you have to swallow a stone.

Kids Called to Trouble Need a Frodo Baggins

BY MARVIN OLASKY
FEBRUARY 17, 1996

The beloved Benjamin and I have just finished our first reading of C.S. Lewis's seven Narnia books. Ben on his fifth birthday, like his three older brothers, started to receive a chapter a night as a bedtime story. If precedent holds, we will roll through them again in three years, but for now Ben is left with memories of all the characters he liked and one, surprisingly, that he did not like—Reepicheep the mouse.

The singling out of Reepicheep startled me because the two-foot-tall talking mouse of the second and third volumes is such a gigantic figure. Reepicheep is a fearless hero, prone to pull out his sword against much larger adversaries. Like our miniature dachshund Wolf (a.k.a. Woofie) who charges trash trucks, yipping furiously, Reepicheep has no problem with self-esteem. What more could a little boy who has to deal with big people ask for?

Upon further probing I learned that Ben was disconcerted because Reepicheep has to pick up the sword at all. In Ben's world, providentially, adults do the big people's job of creating an environment that is safe and nurtures growth, so that the weight is off shoulders too small to bear it. That a small creature had to become a military leader in Narnia seemed strange and slightly threatening.

But what happens when big people don't do their job? What happens when what should be a safe home environment turns into a mansion of aggression? At Boys Town in California (like its famed Omaha parent, now a haven for both boys and girls) I recently met with clearly troubled kids— a ten-year-old who tries to come on sexually to any adult male sitting next to her, a teenager with gang tattoos who cannot sit still in a dress—and wondered how their smashed worlds could be put together again.

There are long-range and short-range answers to that question. Long-range, these kids (like all of us to some degree) will be able to overcome their pasts only if they receive Jesus Christ's assurance that the universe does make sense, even though Satan temporarily rules parts of it. These kids had to harden their hearts incredibly to keep them from being broken, and they need to know that no heart is too hard for Christ to change into a heart of flesh.

In the short run, the kids are helped by entering an environment where the rules are clear and good behavior is rewarded. Boys Town houseparents award points for doing chores, speaking politely, acting courteously, and so on, and demerits for barbaric behavior. The system is so straightforward that kids take to it readily and adults with normal parenting skills can administer it. (One effective houseparent, when asked how and why he hooked up with Boys Town, said truthfully, "I failed as a farmer.")

Crucially, the houseparents are not people of superhuman compassion, nor do they need years of training in social work to do an effective job. They are decent people with church backgrounds and a sound moral sense that God has provided; that, plus three weeks of training in Omaha, equips them to be calm breezes in the lives of children who have previously known gales.

There's a larger lesson to be drawn here: If these ordinary people can do such good work, why can't others? There aren't enough Reepicheeps to go around anyway. Happy is the land that needs no heroes but encourages ordinary people to step up and perform heroic deeds. The federal government now attempts to provide professionals to meet every social need, but Boys Town shows that dedicated amateurs can readily learn and apply a system that helps them do the big people's job of supplying order.

When Ben hits five and a half next month we'll move on to bedtime chapters from J.R.R. Tolkien. Tolkien's great characters Bilbo and Frodo Baggins are not Reepicheeps; they are ordinary hobbits who go off on providential journeys into danger, and in the process receive the pruning all of us need. Hobbits, of course, are only three feet tall, but Bilbo and Frodo are so middle-aged in temperament that I hope Ben will see them as adults going off on God-given quests, not children called to trouble before their time.

When Ben is older he will have adventures of his own, but he's not quite ready to take on those responsibilities yet, and he doesn't have to. For that kindness I thank God and pray that ordinary Bagginses all over this country will give otherwise-helpless children a similar opportunity.

Finally, Some Movement

BY MARVIN OLASKY
AUGUST 17, 1996

Once more unto the breach . . .

Hyperventilating press releases were flying off the fax machines on July 31 and early in August, after President Clinton announced that he would sign this year's welfare reform act. Liberal lobbying groups such as the Children's Defense Fund were proclaiming that Congress and a cowed president were ruthlessly eliminating safeguards for the poor.

The paper blizzard might lead inquiring minds to ask the poverty lobbyists: Why not cut your public relations staffs and use those funds to help people in need? But lapdog newspapers and network news shows instead relayed accusations and skipped by facts. Here are a few questions about the Personal Responsibility and Work Opportunity Reconciliation Act that reporters readily could answer, if they wanted to:

Are the AFDC block grants extremist cuts? Under the new program states will receive the amount they received in fiscal year 1995, or more if their receipts in a previous year were higher.

What if some folks cannot get a job after their five years' eligibility is up? States can exempt up to 20 percent of their total caseloads from the limits, based on individual circumstances. States are also free to use funds from other federal programs to provide services to persons over the five-year limit and to use their own funds to keep folks on the rolls for a lifetime, if they wish.

Are poor people in a state that runs into economic hard times left unprotected? Through a contingency fund, any state with an unemployment rate of 6.5 percent and worsening conditions can receive a 20 percent augmentation of the block grant. States can also tap into a federal revolving loan fund.

Do poor people lose health care coverage? The Act maintains the Medicaid entitlement to families on welfare and provides a year of transitional Medicaid benefits to persons who leave welfare for work.

Do legal immigrants lose all benefits? Veterans of the U.S. military or persons who have worked and paid taxes in the United States for at least ten years retain all benefits, as do refugees. Others become ineligible for food stamps or SSI but can still tap into dozens of other federal programs, including those subsidizing emergency medical services and disaster relief.

Is child-care funding cut? The Act increases the current-law level of mandatory federal child-care funding by $3.5 billion.

Are work requirements for food stamp eligibility onerous? Able-bodied persons between eighteen and fifty with no dependents are to work at least twenty hours per week, eleven months per year. Persons who are mentally or physically unfit for employment, and parents or others who have responsibility for a dependent child, are exempt from the work requirements.

Will changes in welfare increase the number of abortions? Results from states such as New Jersey that have enacted welfare reforms do not indicate any abortion surge. In any event, two wrongs don't make a right; we should be promoting abstinence and adoption, not enabling more teenage sexual activity by guaranteeing cash if pregnancy results.

I could go on with this listing, but I hope my point is clear: The liberal lobbyists are crying wolf. Overall, with this welfare reform, federal welfare spending will still increase by $140 billion over the next six years. Is that a cut?

The Act is incomplete in many ways but hardly onerous, and it even offers states some incentive to improve conditions. States can receive bonus block grants for moving adults from welfare to work or for helping to reduce the rate of out-of-wedlock births without increasing abortion rates.

Why, then, do the publicists and reporters rage? In part, I think, because this welfare reform strikes at two rituals of latter-day liberal religion: (1) Bow to Washington seven times a day; (2) Recite after every meal, "If the federal government doesn't do it, it won't get done."

Could federal welfare changes lead to more poverty? Yes, but only if every other institution in America—state government, local government, philanthropic and charitable organizations, community and religious groups, businesses—fails utterly, and if neither middle-class citizens nor some poor individuals themselves change any aspects of behavior.

Most people think that the possibility of a complete breakdown in all these areas is remote. Those with true faith in the feds do not, and it is from them that the outcry is coming. Nevertheless, it's a pleasure to see some positive change underway and to begin thinking about the next steps.

Land Mines on the Antipoverty Road

BY MARVIN OLASKY
SEPTEMBER 28, 1996

Faith in "faith communities" is sweeping the country's political establishment. That trend is both good news and bad news.

Folks who have read a couple of my recent books might think that I would be overjoyed by this development. I have been suggesting over the past several years that our Washington-centric welfare system should largely be replaced by a new system based on the work of community and religious antipoverty charities.

I've been pointing out that the change is needed particularly because many problems of poverty have spiritual and not just material causes, and yet government is not well equipped to deal with religious matters—nor, given First Amendment concerns, would many Americans want it to.

Last year politicians and their media allies approached the idea of replacing the welfare system with harrumphs: "That will never happen. That's unrealistic." But many conventional reporters have now seen with their own eyes that the concept can work, and as their stories make their way into bureaucratic calculation, a change in tactics is emerging.

Now, the most agile Clintonians are no longer fighting the idea of church involvement in supplying welfare; they are attempting to co-opt it. A recent essay by Henry Cisneros, Secretary of Housing and Urban Development, illuminates the trend. In nineteen pages of a HUD-printed publication entitled *Higher Ground: Faith Communities and Community Building* ("church" is insufficiently pluralistic, "religious institution" sounds too stodgy, so "faith community" is the new hot term), Mr. Cisneros argues that "Faith Communities Have Unique Resources" and "Faith Communities Touch the Soul."

Faith Communities, it appears, have a heritage and a reservoir of respect that other institutions lack, according to Mr. Cisneros. He writes that they are capable of instilling values and moral structure, along with providing "a friend to talk to, or shake hands with, or hug." That's all true and good, as far as it goes: A hug can make a person feel better, for a while.

What's sad, however, is that Mr. Cisneros leaves out the single essential element in promoting true, permanent change. He leaves out God. That word does not make an appearance in his essay. Mr. Cisneros does quote the Bible once, selectively. Isaiah 61:2 deals with "the day of vengeance of our God," but Mr. Cisneros skips by that un-PC concept and quotes 61:4 about how when the Messiah comes (he ignores that part too) Israel "shall repair the waste cities."

The omission of God and the quotation that glorifies HUD rather than God are troublesome. References to God or biblical quotations by themselves would not prove anything. Mr. Cisneros's boss, President Clinton, certainly knows how to twist Scripture for his own uses. But the absence of an effort signifies that this is not even a serious attempt to understand the unique role of religious institutions.

The danger is that the Clinton administration sees churches as potential appendages of the state, useful not for their ability to challenge ungodly beliefs, but for their ability to funnel funds through programs that look like government-issue ones but have greater credibility. Some churches still care enough about God's commands that they will stay clear of such temptations; but others have already entered into a halfway covenant with corruption and may be ready to go all the way.

The excellent bill for poverty-fighting tax credits introduced in Washington by Sen. Dan Coats and Rep. John Kasich also could be twisted. If that legislation gains momentum, liberals will try to amend it to allow taxpayers' money to go directly to political organizing and interest-group lobbying that supposedly helps the poor. As always, the Devil will be in the details.

Some non-Washington programs that are now underway appear to recognize that churches most effectively fight poverty by changing belief, which changes behavior. Governors of Michigan, Virginia, and Mississippi are trying to help churches increase their antipoverty activity. These governors, unlike Mr. Cisneros, appear committed to letting churches be churches, not social agencies.

A key test of the welfare future may come in Texas, where Governor George Bush (a Republican) and Comptroller John Sharp (a Democrat) are both encouraging churches, as well as service clubs, to help get people off welfare. State-promoted programs can work if there is an understanding that churches should fight poverty God's way, not the government's; but whether they will liberate religious institutions or attempt to enslave them remains to be seen.

The way to liberate poor people from the welfare plantation is now apparent, but the path is strewn with land mines.

Thinking Christianly

Pagan People Can't Think

BY JOEL BELZ
JANUARY 22, 1994

Don't ever kid yourself about who's in the driver's seat in our culture war today. Folks who call this a post-Christian society are people given to understatement. It is post-rational as well.

We are a pagan people. Granted, we went for a very long time in this country as something quite other than biblically Christian. But at least we made ample room for the staunch orthodoxy that drove the Pilgrims to these shores; we tended even when we wandered from that orthodoxy to admit that we were wandering. Now we have so lost our compasses that we don't even know we're drifters.

Two items crossing my desk in the last few days reminded me how rootless we have become.

Item 1 is a vigorous column by Ellen Goodman, associate editor of the *Boston Globe*. Mrs. Goodman is a long-time defender of abortion for those who want it and of many other liberal causes.

But last week Mrs. Goodman was saying that enough is enough. She was responding to news that scientists were claiming the ability to take human eggs from aborted female fetuses and use those eggs to help infertile grown women bear children.

"The notion of taking eggs from aborted fetuses is grotesque," says Mrs. Goodman. "But how long is it before someone suggests filling the 'shortage' of eggs in other ways? Will brain-dead or dying females become egg donors the way they are now kidney and liver donors? Will we harvest eggs to conceive our own grandchildren?"

Well, Mrs. Goodman, welcome to the discussion. How is it that you were so late getting here?

It's not exactly news that medical science has been using spare parts from aborted babies for several years. If a little publication like *World* knows that and has published several stories on the subject, how is it that the *Boston Globe* folks find it surprising?

Way back in the days of the Reagan administration, pro-lifers were scorned for suggesting that it might be, well, grotesque, to take brain tissue from an aborted fetus so it could be implanted in an adult suffering from Alzheimer's disease. People such as Mrs. Goodman wondered if we pro-lifers were altogether heartless because we said it was unseemly to traffic in body parts, even for a good cause.

But now she concludes suddenly that "We need some ethical stop signs." Why now? What is so different about helping an Alzheimer's patient and an infertile woman?

Mrs. Goodman has her own answer to that question. Helping infertile women is not a worthy enterprise, she says—at least if the method is to use the eggs of an unborn "mother"—simply because the world is already populated enough. "We live in a world that is bursting at the seams with children," she says, and we simply can't pay that price for children nobody needs.

That's what I mean by a pagan approach. "Before," the columnist sadly concludes, "we depended on nature, the life cycles, the human body, to determine our limits. Now we must depend on the heart and the brain. At times, they seem like much less reliable organs."

In other words, the associate editor of the *Boston Globe* doesn't have a clue when she should insist on erecting an ethical stop sign and when she should scorn someone else for wanting to do exactly the same thing.

Item 2, meanwhile, is a lavish new coffee-table book from the Smithsonian Institution titled *Timelines of the Ancient World*. The $49.95, 250-page volume is, in the words of its own subtitle, "A Visual Chronology from the Origins of Life to A.D. 1500." The impressive editorial staff is headed by Chris Scarre, a Ph.D. scholar who edits the twice-yearly *Cambridge Archaeological Journal*.

I wasn't surprised, in looking through the book, to see the endless assumptions of the evolutionary origins of humankind around which the book is structured. Nor was it startling to see the very politically correct emphasis on a great variety of nationalities, cultures, and religions that didn't get much ink in the ancient history textbooks I studied thirty years ago.

You do have to wonder why in a comprehensive book on this topic, however, Alexander the Great and Alfred the Great are both in the index under "A" while Abraham is not. Da Gama (Vasco), Darius I, and Darwin (Charles) are the first three entries under "D," but they are not followed by Israel's greatest king, David. Under "M," Marcus Aurelius gets a line, and so does Mithradates II, but not Moses, the Jewish lawgiver.

So you don't get lost along the way, the book's editors have been kind to let you know what general time frame you're in on any given page. Chapter 1 sketches the brief period between "4,600—1 Million Years Ago." The Ice Ages get their due in Chapter 2, and Chapter 3 covers the "First Modern Humans" during the period between 100,000 and 35,000 years ago.

It's in the big title for Chapter 4 that the plot thickens. "Crossing to America" is, of course, pre-Christopher Columbus, and the editors underline that by putting the dates in big type: 33,000-13,000 B.C.

What on earth could those initials B.C. mean? From that page on you see them recurring in both titles and text as you speed down the timeline toward more familiar eras. The ice thaws before 8,000 B.C. The Ubaid culture built temples about 6,000 B.C. People learned to farm and hunt by 5,000 B.C. Mesopotamian city-states prospered between 4,000 and 2,000 B.C.

The crescendo picks up as the pages turn. What will happen when these B.C.numbers run out—which occurs, you know, when you go from largest to smallest. In this book, it happens on page 162, where the big type at the top announces: "100 A.D.." But look as you will at the little type, both here and throughout the book, you'll never find so much as a passing reference to Jesus Christ, the Lord of all the ages. The whole book is measured around him—as of course all reality is—but he doesn't get a mention.

Could it be a mere oversight in a magnificent book that gives painstaking attention to thousands of other details? If you believe that, you might also be hopeful that Ellen Goodman is about to start a new pro-life chapter in Boston.

What we have are people who are trying desperately to construct their world—its ethical systems, its history, and everything else that's important—apart from the God who put it all here. It's bad enough, as America and many other countries have done, to try to deprive God of his full glory and to seek much of that credit for themselves. It's so much worse to try to crowd him out altogether. We live more and more in a bizarre never-never land that has little in common with the reality of the Bible.

Balance on the High Wire

BY   JOEL   BELZ
MARCH   31,   1986

A man came to our town two weeks ago and advertised boldly in the local paper that he was going to defy the laws of God—in public.

Well, it wasn't exactly the way it sounds. The man was a tightrope walker with Ringling Brothers, Barnum and Bailey Circus. What the newspaper ad really said was that for $9 I could watch this fellow defy the laws of gravity. I'm not at all sure the acrobat knows that God controls gravity.

I didn't go to the circus, but the acrobat's claim set me thinking. What with all the lawbreaking going on in the world today, why would someone set out to break another one of God's laws so gratuitously?

The fact is, of course, that there are two distinct categories of God's laws. There are the ones like "don't lie," "don't steal," and "don't commit adultery"—laws that seem all too easy to break. Then there is that other set of laws like "2 + 3 = 5," "yellow + blue = green," and "two solid objects can't occupy the same space at the same time"—laws that some of us work pretty hard to break, but that seem to get more and more certain as time goes on.

That's where appearances are deceiving, in several ways. We all know (even non-Christians know it) that when you break that second set of laws, you end up getting broken yourself; but we suppose that somehow with the right kind of cleverness we can sneak around the first set of laws and get off scot-free. It doesn't work that way at all. The evidence is that in the long run, on balance, we would be far better off ignoring the second set of rules and observing the first. The damage we would do would be severe, but not so long-lasting.

In fact, human misery is summarized in our rebellion against both sets of laws. Most of us would break even the second set of God's physical laws more regularly except that somehow we discover more quickly that life doesn't work as well when we do. Without that short tether, we'd be just as messed up there as we are with God's moral laws.

Part of our task as Christians is to discover, and then proclaim to others, how God's overall rules for life—both moral and physical—are designed to bring harmony and balance in all of life. This is true for us as individuals, as families, as communities, as nations, and in the world at large. Looking at the news, a primary function of *World* magazine, makes it easy to see what we're doing wrong. Looking at God's Word is the best way to discover how we're supposed to do it right.

About that acrobat—he wasn't really breaking God's laws. Whether he knew it or not, he was observing them. That's why he kept his balance—something people paid to watch him do.

AIDS and God's Mercy

BY JOEL BELZ
JUNE 22, 1987

Theologians might argue a long time over which comes first: God's mercy in forgiving those who repent or the repentance that leads to his mercy. I know my own stubborn heart well enough to be certain that no repentance would ever occur unless it were first prompted by his mercy.

However that may be, this is a time in human history to speak forcefully about the relationship between God's mercy and our own repentance. The important truth is this: You can never talk about one without also talking about the other.

Only a year ago (and even less) it was considered harsh to say that AIDS might properly be construed as God's big stick. But when people right around you start dropping dead from the disease, you begin moving from polite posturing to a considerably more desperate yell for help: "Who's trying to get my attention?"

God is not only trying to get people's attention—he's getting it, whether or not those folks recognize God as the source of the message.

The big question is: What will people do with his message when they get it?

To answer that question honestly, we need to remind ourselves that if AIDS is one of God's big sticks, he has lots of little sticks that he uses first. And they are not particularly different in kind. I have said in this space before that AIDS and the common cold have the same ancestry; they are both results of the Fall. But AIDS and the common cold also ultimately have the same purpose; they are both there to call us back to God, to remind us of our own human frailty, to turn us from self-reliance, and to prompt us to cast ourselves anew on God's mercy. The common cold does it gently, while AIDS does it almost viciously. It's the difference between a gentle scolding and capital punishment.

In stressing that AIDS and a cold differ only in severity, not in kind, we should see that both are essentially acts of God's mercy. How? Because both stop us from proceeding in a harmful direction and turn us in a helpful one.

Strange as it may seem to do so, consider the gentleness of AIDS. The very nature of the disease, when you stop to think about it, is a passive rather than an active attack on the body. God says, in effect, "All right, watch this. You're presuming to tell me you can make up your own rules for your body as you go along? Then I'll make you fully responsible for yourself. And that full responsibility you now have for yourself includes protecting yourself from other diseases. Until you listen to me, it's your job—not mine anymore—to make yourself immune to other harmful illnesses." That, you see, is what an immune deficiency is all about.

Now, wouldn't anybody in his right mind pay attention to such a warning? Yet, by the tens of thousands people are ignoring it. So full of confidence are they, so proud, and so arrogant, that they remain quite sure they can make it on their own. They will not turn, they will not listen, they will not acknowledge in any sense that they've been on the wrong track.

So now you answer: Whose is the next move? Is it time for God to move in on a worldwide catastrophe and show his mercy? Or is it time for human beings to concede that he's already done so, knuckle under, and change our ways?

All apart from AIDS, I've come in recent days to be more attentive to God's little sticks—the gentle reminders he uses to get me back on his path. The little sticks are literal "aids" to obedience, and I'd just as soon keep seeing them in small rather than capital letters.

What Did Jeremiah Mean?

BY JOEL BELZ
DECEMBER 11, 1993

Our little mountain city of Asheville, N.C., is rated as one of the best places in America to call home. Normally that's the case—and hundreds of *World* readers who have visited here can confirm that boast.

But for the last few weeks, Asheville has suffered the indignity of having a quiet and long-festering problem become a little too public. We have an outdated and (some say) mismanaged public water system that is falling apart at the seams. And because of that, visitors who stop in Asheville might well discover that instead of getting a glass of sparkling mountain water, they get a glassful of something far less gleaming and perhaps even a little bit gritty. Lack of rain in recent months means our reservoirs are low, and sediment tends to get into the system.

Indeed, when some *World* subscribers visited us in October, the very fine restaurant where we took them told us there would be no coffee that evening because the water in the city lines might damage the coffeemaker. I didn't have the nerve to tell the manager he could simply have heated the water coming out of the pipes and persuaded some people that it was coffee.

From the time of Noah's flood until the 1993 rampage of the Mississippi River—with plenty of other examples in between—God has used water to make people stop and think. It's a great attention-getter, whether through shortage or oversupply.

The prophet Jeremiah presents this stark picture of drought:

> *Judah mourns,*
> *her cities languish;*
> *they wail for the land,*
> *and a cry goes up from Jerusalem.*
> *The nobles send their servants for water;*
> *they go to the cisterns*
> *but find no water.*

> *They return with their jars unfilled;*
>   *dismayed and despairing,*
>   *they cover their heads.*
> *The ground is cracked*
>   *because there is no rain in the land;*
> *the farmers are dismayed*
>   *and cover their heads.*
> *Even the doe in the field*
>   *deserts her newborn fawn*
>   *because there is no grass.*
> *Wild donkeys stand on the barren heights*
>   *and pant like jackals;*
> *their eyesight fails*
>   *for lack of pasture.*
>   *—Jeremiah 14:2-6*

Now let me suggest four possible responses to such reports—whether those reports come from a major prophet like Jeremiah, from a reporter for the Asheville *Citizen-Times*, or from the Hannibal (Mo.) *Courier-Post*.

Response number 1 is what I call the Pharaoh response. It is, in effect, to curse your luck and to harden your heart. No literal cursing perhaps, but there are plenty of ways to curse figuratively. People do it regularly when it rains—and when it doesn't rain. It might be so mild as calling yourself "unlucky" for not being able to golf because of a thunderstorm. For others, God's revelation of himself through meteorology produces much more negative, and sometimes more blasphemous, responses. In all these cases God shows himself—and people's response is to distance themselves rather than to draw closer to him.

Response number 2 is simply to say quite sincerely and quite humbly, "OK, God—you've got my attention. I admit I've ignored you too much. I confess I've set my own agenda without reference to what you want in my life. Now I'm reminded that you're in charge, that you're much bigger and more powerful than I am. I'm reminded that anytime you want, you could wash me away, or you could make me gasp for a single drop of refreshing water. I'm sorry it took this drought [or this flood] to remind me of that, and I'm going to try hard to remember in the future that you come first."

Response number 3 is to spiritualize the reminder, or to make a metaphor of it. Water is, of course, a recurring symbol through the whole Bible. Water sometimes means judgment. For Noah, however, the very water that drowned the scoffers lifted him up to deliverance. Sometimes in the Bible water purifies; that is its rich symbolism in the sacrament of baptism. So when God either sends or withholds rain, it is possible for us to respond with any of these metaphorical ideas in mind. "Let it rain," we might cry. "Wash away the dustiness and the dirtiness of my sin, and refresh me by letting me drink deeply of the good things you provide for those who hear you and turn to you in faith."

After all that, response number 4 may strike you as distinctly non-spiritual and mundane. Response number 4 is to reflect on the technical, meteorological, scientific, sociological, economic, or political reasons for the shortage or the overabundance of water. To put it quite simply, this fourth response is to ask the question, Have we been good stewards of the water supply? Have we managed it well? For example, there is evidence here in Asheville that for many years the infrastructure of the water supply system has been badly managed—that tax revenues that ought to have gone for updating the pipelines were in fact siphoned off for other causes. That is poor stewardship. It may, conversely, also be poor stewardship to build houses and businesses in the Mississippi River flood plain. Crises such as droughts and floods remind us of such poor stewardship.

So, which is the right reading of Jeremiah and the daily newspaper? Clearly, none of us wants to react like Pharaoh. But of the other three responses, is there one that's especially on target in God's eyes?

To the contrary, the beauty of God's revelation to us is that all three positive responses are appropriate. Partly, he just wants us to redirect our attention to him after it has wandered, and he uses floods, droughts, and other events in our lives to accomplish just that end. He also wants us to understand the eternal significance of our relationship to him, and to that end virtually everything around us can be properly construed as a metaphor or an object lesson of important principles we are supposed to keep in mind. But we are also living in the here and now—a present reality that is also God-created and that he once called very good. Just because we have marred it with sin doesn't mean we're now justified in continued sloppy stewardship. Part of our response when we hear about things being out of balance is, in a very practical and literal sense, to help restore them to the balance God first created. We bring glory to him when we do that.

Read your Bible and your newspaper at all three levels—and look for new dimensions as well. And rejoice in the richness of the fabric of God's truth.

Mother Nature, Father God

BY JOEL BELZ
FEBRUARY 5, 1994

After another whole week of listening to mystical, evasive comments about the apparent anger of "Mother Nature," it's time for Christians everywhere to say in emphatic terms, "The doctrine of creation matters."

The problem is that so few Christians really believe that anymore; they simply can't say those words with any gumption. For a generation now, evangelicals have increasingly swallowed the line that what we believe about origins is really just about the same as what everyone else believes—except that we think God controlled the process. Leading evangelical colleges quietly but efficiently persuade thousands of students that theistic evolution is a more sophisticated and less embarrassing explanation of origins than what we learned as beginners in Sunday school. Those who still hold to the quaint idea that God made everything in six twenty-four-hour days are regularly made to feel as if they should also be speaking Elizabethan English.

All this has a practical effect on everyday behavior and conversation. The day after the big earthquake in California, while waiting in line at the bank, the women in front of me and I were watching a cat just outside the window. The cat sat crouched beneath a bush, eyeing a bird above her as only a feline can.

"I have two cats," the woman told me. "But I don't let them play with birds. Mice, moles, shrews—OK. They can gobble them up to their hearts' content. But no birds. Can you believe some people get a thrill out of watching a cat catch and eat a bird?"

Well, no, I can't—unless maybe it's a lion in Kenya on the prowl for a buzzard. But I was puzzled, and still am, at the source of our double standard. "Do you suppose," I asked the woman at the bank, "that God built that into his creation—that he planned that we would put a higher value on canaries than we do on mice? Or is that something we came up with on our own?" The woman's response was a silent blank stare, as if I had suddenly started speaking in a dialect from remote Tibet.

I had, of course, broken a profound social taboo. Tom Brokaw and Peter Jennings can talk all evening long, as both of them did, about the wrath of Mother Nature. A serious quote got wide play in the media to the effect that Mother Earth was finally getting angry at all the abuse and pollution human beings have piled on her in recent years and, through the earthquake, was saying bluntly, "Enough!"

But nary a word about God's role in all this. Just imagine the red faces on every side if someone were to explore seriously the possibility that the one who put the planets in their orbits was rattling one of them just a bit.

The problem is not, however, the difference between "religious" people like us and "nonreligious" people like network news anchors. The problem is that "religious" people like us have forfeited the whole idea that God is intimately involved with his creation—at least when it comes time for public debate and discourse. We may claim to believe it theoretically, but our theoretical convictions do not pervade our everyday assumptions and conversation.

That happens, you see, when you set aside the idea of a God who says, "Let there be light"—and suddenly, by the word of his power, there is light. If it takes 37 billion years for light to discover how to find its way across the heavens, it doesn't make much sense to talk about a God who can shake southern California for twenty-six seconds early on a January morning.

It bothers people profoundly to have to think about God's involvement in Hurricane Andrew, in the Blizzard of '93, in the Mississippi River floods, and in the great earthquake of 1994. But the big reason that's so disturbing to folks is that they've never joined Job as he sat and marveled at God the Creator. They've never worshiped a God who has ultimate power.

A good test when comparing theories of creation is simply this: Which gives God the greatest glory? I learned this indirectly as a nine-year-old when I tried one time to put on an amateur magic show for my parents, my brothers and sisters, and my neighbors. Getting to a particularly crucial point where I had neither prepared nor practiced well enough, I asked everyone to shut their eyes for just a moment. They were kind and did so, but I knew I'd blown it. The glory of a grand performance was ruined.

In similar fashion the difference between a God who snaps his fingers and says, "Let the dry land appear" and a God who takes several million years to allow glaciers to carve it all out in random fashion—that difference is profound.

Last summer's floods lasted a couple of months. The blizzard earlier in the year lasted a day or two. Hurricane Andrew came and went in a few hours. The earthquake two weeks ago lasted just a few seconds. In a sense the lesson is this: The shorter the performance, the more rapt will be the audience's attention. People are impressed when a lot of power is unleashed in a short time.

By forfeiting the story of creation the way most of us learned it, we've forfeited the stage now to talk about the same God who set it all in motion. If people find it hard to believe in the one, it will be hard for them as well to believe in the other.

But they'd better learn to believe in such a God. If he's big and powerful enough to make it in the first place, he's also big and powerful enough to shake it up now and then. The ultimate message for men and women is that he's also big and powerful enough to break it as well—something he promises he will do just before he makes all things new. When he does that, the evidence is strong it's going to happen in the twinkling of an eye.

Birth Is Always Just a Start

BY JOEL BELZ
JUNE 4, 1994

A week never goes by without our mailbag spitting out at least one letter urging us to leave behind our preoccupation with "all these secular things" and to get back to the "simple Gospel of Jesus Christ."

"If you'd spend your time urging people to turn to Jesus," one letter-writer from Texas told me last week, "you might not appear to be so sophisticated—but you'd do a lot more good. I get the impression you're trying to skip what Paul called 'the foolishness of preaching.'"

So let me say plainly: I do not dismiss that criticism as the naive protest of a narrow-minded fundamentalist. Jesus repeatedly called people back to basics—back to the fundamentals, if you will. He told one of his most sophisticated questioners that he simply had to be born again.

The core of that process of being born again is to reject our habit of self-dependence and to transfer our dependence to God. To be born again is to admit that we are weak and broken and sinful, and to confess that God is powerful and whole and perfect. Most specifically, it is to understand that God's power and wholeness and perfection are personified in the God-man, Jesus, and that God is willing to count Jesus' righteousness on our behalf when we finally tell him that our own righteousness is not good enough—that we need to be bailed out from our own failure.

Such is the beginning of the Gospel. Without some form of that basic understanding, no person has any right to expect to walk with God, either in this life or in eternity. It absolutely has to start with this, and it always has to start personally.

But just because the Gospel starts there doesn't mean it ends there.

The birth of a baby is exciting, but no one really wants a baby to stay a baby forever. Birth is exciting because it means a new person has come on the scene, full of potential. So while *World* rejoices whenever a man or woman or boy or girl drops self-trust and starts trusting in Christ, we see that exciting moment only as a profound beginning. If the new birth doesn't happen, there's no new person in Christ. But the new birth, like natural birth, is still just a beginning.

That's why Jesus' final instruction was to go out to teach "everything I have commanded you" (Matthew 28:20). The implications of this thing we call Christ's Gospel are profound and far-reaching.

In one sense, this may all seem very complex. But in fact it's pretty simple. God says to us, in effect: "If you expect to trust me for the details of your invisible, long-term existence, you might as well get used to that process by trusting me also for the visible, short term as well. Yes, the Gospel is about spiritual and eternal matters. But to prove its trustworthiness in those realms, I want you also to see how trustworthy I am in the realms you're used to living in."

So the good news of the Gospel, we discover, has implications for the here and now. It has implications for morality and education, for politics and justice, for art and music, for business and finance. In all those areas and more, God calls his children to new perspectives that, like the new birth itself, may at first seem foolish. But the more we keep exploring them, and the more we learn to trust God's ways in all those areas of life, the more he makes sense to us.

That's one way of describing what we call a "Christian worldview."

To go exploring in all these nitty-gritty areas of life is never a denial of the basic Gospel where we all must start. It is rather the logical extension of that magnificent journey.

Who Are People of Faith?

BY JOEL BELZ
AUGUST 27, 1994

I'm not sure where the term *people of faith* came from, but here's my vote against it.

I've heard the phrase used increasingly in recent weeks to refer, I suppose, to people who openly confess a sort of trust in some higher power. The facile description seems to include Christians (both Protestant and Catholic, both evangelical and liberal, both fervent and nominal), Jews, Muslims, and a number of others too numerous and diverse to mention.

The Christian Coalition, in a widely publicized report a few days ago, referred to "a highly partisan campaign against religious folk launched by the national Democratic party." The report chastised the Jewish Anti-Defamation League for "lending its name to this campaign against people of faith. . . ."

Such terminology, however, fails totally in making two important distinctions—and is therefore both too broad and too narrow at the same time. It assumes first that all *people of faith* belong in the same category— that what makes them alike is more important than any differences among them. And it assumes, secondly, that there is some critical distinction between so-called *people of faith* and *people without faith*.

Both those assumptions are wrong.

Trying to cram all *people of faith* into the same box is at best a meaningless exercise. At worst, it's like taking 1,000 plants—some edible, some poisonous—and stressing that their most important characteristic is that they all have roots. Never mind who dies as a result of such superficial classification.

At least two critical questions must be asked before a reference to *faith* means anything at all: What's the purpose of the faith? And who's the object of that faith?

Part of what distinguishes Christian *faith* is that it has to do with life and death. That separates it from any mere system of Norman Vincent Pealeish improvement that sees faith only as some sort of confidence-building picker-upper, something that will add a little zing to your optimism. Biblical faith grapples with radical rather than superficial problems. It's a desperate confession that we are in such terrible straits that we need outside help. It's a transfer of trust from ourselves to someone else for everything that's important.

So for starters, if a person doesn't think of faith in such radical terms—if that person doesn't think of faith quite literally as *saving faith*—then it doesn't really matter that he or she associates with other *people of faith*. It's a meaningless association.

And second, it's essential to ask: Who is this faith in? People always answer that in one of three ways:

1. The God of the Bible.

2. Somebody or something else.

3. A combination of the God of the Bible and somebody or something else.

Biblically and historically, Christianity has always declared that any fudging on this matter constitutes error. The apostle Paul wasn't terribly ecumenical when he said flatly that if anyone came bearing any message other than hope exclusively in Jesus Christ, that person should be considered "accursed" or "eternally condemned" (Galatians 1:8). Some such heretics came pretty close to the truth but still missed—and Paul didn't give them the fuzzy title *people of faith*.

Yes, this gets down to fine points. Point #1 above is precisely what separates evangelical Christians from Jews. Who, they ask each other, is the God of the Bible? Evangelical Christians, by definition, insist that Jesus is that God. Most Jews still reject that claim. Point #3 has historically divided evangelical Protestants from Roman Catholics. The Reformation insisted that faith alone—not faith plus works—is the basis of salvation from sin, but diligent Catholics still take issue with that distinction.

In any case, Christians don't serve their own cause well, even in a secular setting, when they blur the definition of the word *faith*. It may be fine (and even necessary in some circumstances) to find things that fundamentalist Baptists and Mormons and Orthodox Jews and Black Muslims and liberal Presbyterians and New Agers all hold in common. But please don't call it *faith*—which usually is the very thing that separates them.

Yet if faith is defined too broadly that way, it is also defined much too narrowly by those who talk about *people of faith*. For in fact every human being who has ever lived has had faith in something. That's what some philosophers mean when they say that all of life is religious. Everything we do is a sorting out of where different ones of us put our ultimate confidence.

It is possible, to be sure, to classify these different kinds of ultimate confidence up and down a spectrum. You might start at the top with ultimate confidence in the Christ of the New Testament. Then you'd speak more broadly of confidence in an Old Testament but not-yet-triune God. And then you move down the scale—to all other monotheistic deities (like that of Islam), to polytheistic but outside-the-universe gods, to polytheistic but inside-the-universe gods, to animist gods, to plant gods, etc.

But what do you do then with complex systems such as New-Age theology, which borrows freely from all of the above? Are New Agers *people of faith*? And what of people who devote their whole lives to material success, or to the gods of science, or the goddesses of education, or even those whose God is something as wonderful as their own children? The faith of all these folks is often not just profound but zealous. The trust they exhibit puts to shame the trust many evangelicals have in Jesus. So, are they *people of faith*?

I know the Christian Coalition and others who use the term *people of faith* mean well. And I share their outrage at those who in public discourse take such delight in attacking various groups that believe American society should take God's laws more seriously than it now does.

But those are temporary issues. The ultimate issues have to do with where we put our final trust. If in our zeal to resolve temporary issues we do anything that blurs those that are ultimate, we do an eternal disservice to everyone.

God's Two Voices

BY   JOEL   BELZ
SEPTEMBER   16 ,   1995

Which did you pick up first this morning—your daily newspaper or your Bible?

I used to think that was a phony and diversionary question, asked only by pietists eager to show how holy they were compared to the rest of us. But lately I've concluded there's legitimacy to the test.

Like too many of us, the noteworthy Swiss theologian Karl Barth pulled his punches when he answered the question. The serious Christian, he said, should read with a Bible in one hand and the daily newspaper in the other. That way, you can see what God is doing in the world but constantly refine your perspective in the light of God's eternal truth.

I think I understand what Dr. Barth was saying; I've argued in that same direction myself. But I also think it's dangerous advice, for it implies there's some kind of equivalence between the two kinds of revelation.

It is true that God reveals himself in two primary ways. One vehicle is the Bible. The other, my father used to remind me very simply, is everything else. All God's creation and all God's providence are just as surely an expression of his voice as is the Bible.

But saying that is not the same as saying that all those other expressions of his voice are as clear as the Bible or that they speak with the same force and authority. Hurricane Luis was a strong expression of God's providence, but the meaning of Hurricane Luis was much more ambiguous than are the words of the book of Romans.

So yes, you can and should discern the hand of God at work when you read your daily newspaper. But no, you should never pretend that what you are reading in that newspaper—even if you discern the hand of God in what you read—comes with the same authority that the Bible carries.

Which brings me back to this morning's choice between my Bible and my newspaper.

We Christians find it far too easy to suppose we are somehow pre-equipped to think Christianly about everything going on around us. We think we know the main drift of biblical morality and biblical thinking and are therefore ready to pick up the paper and know—almost intuitively— what a biblical perspective is on all those issues.

We kid ourselves. Yes, it is important that we nurture "the mind of Christ" within ourselves—and that does happen through lifelong disciplines. But it doesn't happen all at once. And because we are in a profoundly sinful world, that which we carefully develop through the years is also challenged regularly by the evil one and therefore tends to be torn down.

That's why all of us need to be infused frequently with the life-giving discernment of God's special revelation in the Bible. Better to try to keep up your physical well-being without eating every day than to keep up your powers of godly discernment without daily recourse to God's very words and instruction for his children.

Granted, the precise order in which we take our different kinds of nourishment may be a matter of personal preference.

But nutritionists still recommend a healthy breakfast! And personal experience from God's saints through all ages—including David the Psalmist (Psalm 143:8)—suggests that an early start with God's Word is key. Here are three reasons that is so:

1. It is a daily symbolic statement of what is most important.

2. In practical terms, what you do first tends to get done; what you put off competes with other obligations and tends to get bumped from the schedule.

3. What you do first tends to define the rest of the day.

That third point is key. It is essential when you pick up your newspaper that you have already have the mind of Christ. That happens best when you are already saturated with the very words of God as recorded in the history recorded by Moses, the poetry of God's beleaguered people, the warnings of the prophets, the great news of the Gospels, and the encouragement of the apostles to early Christians. Those words will shape your life—every day.

I mention the morning newspaper because it's the way so many people start their day. I have myself for too many years, and my guess is that many *World* readers, as news junkies, do the same. Some of you, heaven forbid, may even start the day with *World*!

Don't. Start instead with that which defines everything else. Everything else, including *World*, will make a lot more sense.

Ninety-nine Irrelevant Sheep

BY JOEL BELZ
MARCH 9, 1996

Which brings more delight to the inscrutable heart of God—the child of his who obeys quite precisely, living a compliant life of genuinely humble and fruitful service, or the rebel son who, only after kicking over the traces and thumbing his nose at his Creator, finally returns in humility and repentance and begs to have things set straight?

Biblically, the answer might seem a little confusing. Take Matthew 18:13, for example. Speaking of the man who at last discovers his wandering sheep, Jesus is quite specific: "And if he finds it, I tell you the truth, he is happier about that one sheep than about the ninety-nine that did not wander off."

Or turn to Luke 15 and read about all the emotion surrounding the return of the prodigal son. The Lord says that while the boy was still a good ways off, "his father saw him and was filled with compassion for him; he ran to his son, threw his arms around him and kissed him." Indeed, the response was so overwhelming that the older son became jealous of his father's attention.

Taken superficially, these well-known stories—along with dozens of other biblical accounts—might seem to encourage us all to do exactly what the apostle Paul mentions in his epistles. Maybe we should all go off on a long and sinful binge, just so everyone can watch God rejoice when he finally straightens us out and welcomes us back into his loving arms.

Maybe—except that Paul is extraordinarily blunt in his response to such a suggestion: "God forbid," he says (Romans 6:2, KJV).

When you stop to think about it, that huge enterprise we call *the kingdom of God* might well be divided into two primary kinds of tasks. On the one hand, big chunks of time and money and other resources are being invested in fencing in and tethering the ninety-nine sheep, making sure they keep behaving properly and never run away. On the other hand, perhaps even more massive expenditures of lives and dollars and energies are regularly being targeted at rescue operations for lost sheep.

Who could deny the propriety in a biblical scheme of things for both kinds of enterprise? Who would deny the importance of either? When budget time comes at your local church, nobody likes to have to choose between support for the youth pastor on the one hand and the local rescue mission on the other. Isn't there a proper place in the budget for both Christian education and foreign missions?

Except that my first question was a bit different. There I asked which of these two kinds of activity brings greatest delight not to us, but to the heart of God.

The answer involves a surprise. The ninety-nine sheep never really even existed. The prodigal's older brother didn't exist either—at least not as the proper, well-behaved boy we've always imagined. In that sense, he was just a prop for the story.

Indeed, there's really nobody at all like that. "For all have sinned and fall short of the glory of God" (Romans 3:23). Jesus was withering the Pharisees with irony when he spoke of the ninety-nine sheep and the older son. "Go ahead and pretend," he was saying. "But it's only pretense."

In the end, God's huge household is made up of just one category of people. All of us are sinners who have gotten tired, or are getting tired, of our sin.

For some, that sin was flagrant and open, like that of the prodigal. For others, it was secret and quiet, like that of the older brother. But for everyone who now calls himself or herself a child of God, the reality of that sin has at some point gotten so heavy that finally we had to turn to Jesus and say, "I'm no good. Help me, please."

So neither are there really two different kinds of activity in God's kingdom. There's not this one task of trying to spruce up some folks who are already pretty good, and another task of radically straightening out and reforming the rest who are unspeakably bad.

There's only one task, and that is repeatedly spelling out the great grace of God to all groups of people. The challenge of the Sunday school teacher is ultimately just like that of the counselor at the rescue mission—helping both the class of fourth graders and the group of winos and derelicts understand how weak they are by themselves and how great are the resources of God for everything they ever hope to accomplish. The task of your pastor when he preaches to you next Sunday is just like that of the volunteer in the crisis pregnancy center the next day—to remind both you and the distraught young mother that if you depend on your own strength, you will always be broken, but that you can lay that brokenness at the feet of Jesus. He has the power to take care of it.

Pretending we are good and that we have something special to offer God does nothing to make him happy. It is instead an insult to him.

When and if God's people get that straight, right in our own circles, we may be a bit more ready to take on the woes of the rest of a terribly broken world. Until then we might come across like the ninety-nine sheep and the older brother—off to the side of where the real action is taking place.

Journalism and the Media

Fairness in the Media? Forget It

BY JOEL BELZ
SEPTEMBER 19, 1992

Not since this world began has there been so much talk about the bias in the public media—especially the big TV networks and major news magazines.

Complaints about bias always pick up, of course, during an election year. What's extraordinary this fall is the acknowledgment even of some traditionally liberal observers that matters have gotten out of hand. "The media are incredibly pro-Clinton," says Mickey Kaus of *The New Republic*. "I get embarrassed watching the news these days. Every story is twisted against Bush." And last week, ABC-TV's Peter Jennings reported on his evening newscast that he'd heard a great deal of similar criticism.

I have a theory about all this, however—a theory not terribly popular with people who are media bashers, but consistent nonetheless with what the Bible teaches about human nature.

The theory is simply that the media haven't gotten a whole lot worse than they used to be. The society they represent and report to has.

Central to most people's perception of the media's obligation is what we've always called objectivity or fairness. And central to the concept of objectivity is the even more basic concept of truth.

But truth in the modern age is in short supply. Even most Republicans, who understandably are complaining most loudly these days about bias in the news, don't really believe in truth, if by that we mean non-relativistic

absolutes. Even most Republicans, for example, shrink from saying dog-
matically that there's only one way to God. That, they fear, might offend
a Jewish or an Islamic friend. Most Republicans also shy away from abso-
lutism about abortion; only a bold few assert that it's always wrong. All
of us have been so desensitized that we run scared when we bump into
people who see things in terms of black and white rather than polite
shades of gray.

So what does that have to do with fairness? Precisely this: When you
have relativized everything else in life, even the things you can't imagine
relativizing are relativized.

We like to think, of course, that a basic concept such as fairness
should be possible in a society even after it has rejected something as dog-
matic as Jesus-centered biblical theology. And to a certain extent, God's
common grace does allow even the pagan mind to think now and then
about fairness. But that is more a leftover benefit, a residual blessing, than
something you can count on.

In the end, "every good and perfect gift is from above" (James 1:17).
And soon as we start thinking we can structure a society that has even the
trappings of something like fairness after jettisoning God's truth and
God's laws, we have taken off on what the Bible calls "vain imaginations."
It simply isn't possible.

So there should be no surprise now if the media forget about fairness
in reporting, just as there should be no surprise that we've forgotten about
faithfulness in marriage and about nighttime safety on the streets of our
big cities. The virtues and delights human beings crave will all prove more
and more elusive as our society denies more and more explicitly and more
and more emphatically the source of all virtue and delight.

Reports coming in the last few months from the former Soviet Union
describe the grisly mistrust, the advantage-taking, the loss of civility. That
wasn't just because of totalitarianism. The true root of that awful lifestyle
was the Godlessness of the regime—and it's important in this case to use
a capital G.

Sooner or later it comes down to crooked umpires and supermarkets
that cheat you. It comes to airlines that only pretend to inspect their planes
and dairies that dilute their milk. On the way to such a happy future, why
should we be surprised at networks and magazines who don't know what
fairness is?

Thrum, Thrum: Media Soothing

BY MARVIN OLASKY
DECEMBER 9, 1995

One of the great scenes in C.S. Lewis's Chronicles of Narnia comes in book 4, *The Silver Chair*, when the evil Queen of Underland tries to lull the heroes into sleepiness. The queen's main tool is a mandolin that she plays with "a steady, monotonous thrumming that you didn't notice after a few minutes. But the less you noticed it, the more it got into your brain and your blood. This also made it hard to think."

We are hearing a similar kind of thrumming during the budget battles in Washington. During round 1 last month, ABC, CBS, and NBC ran twenty-nine evening news stories concerning the partial federal government shutdown and the reasons behind it; but not one of them, according to the Media Research Center, mentioned the actual levels of spending that were at issue. Thrum, thrum. Not a single story pointed out that President Clinton's ten-year balanced budget plan was likely to leave us with annual deficits greater than $200 billion. Thrum, thrum.

In *The Silver Chair*, the queen regularly checks the results of her thrumming; today liberal journalists take constant public opinion polls to measure the effect of theirs. The question in a *Washington Post*/ABC News poll, "Do you approve or disapprove of the way Clinton is handling the dispute?" could more accurately have been restated as, How are we doing? Has our entrancing coverage convinced you that the deficit-enhancers are right? Have your senses been dulled? Thrum, thrum: Look at poll numbers, not budget figures.

In *The Silver Chair*, the Queen of Underland's enchantment makes the heroes discount their own experience and knowledge: How can you be sure there is a world on the surface of the earth? Liberal journalists throw the poll numbers at those who are fighting for a balanced budget: How can you be right if the American people say you are wrong? Thrum, thrum. Since Americans want us to get on with business as usual, those who demand change must be doing it out of personal petulance. Thrum, thrum.

In *The Silver Chair*, the ever-pessimistic character Puddleglum saves the day by deliberately burning his foot in a fire: Pain breaks the spell. Americans need to be awakened also, but the change is unlikely to be as sudden. The thrumming, after all, occurs not only during budget battles, but on any issue in which Bible-based values challenge liberal humanism.

Bonnie Erbe of PBS, trying on November 3 to minimize the damage to the pro-abortion position brought about by gruesomely accurate descriptions of partial-birth abortions, asked, "Aren't most medical procedures, when you describe them in detail, pretty disgusting? Isn't, for example, the production of veal, when you describe it in detail, and how people eat meat, when they crunch down on the flesh of living beings, formerly living beings with their teeth? Isn't that pretty gruesome?" Thrum, thrum.

Newsweek writer Jonathan Alter, dealing with reports of Clinton adultery, argued that the Clintons "rightly complain that they have been punished for keeping their family intact. Had they simply gotten divorced, Clinton's sex life wouldn't have been an issue." Thrum, thrum.

And on the question of bias itself, Dan Rather said, "Most reporters don't know whether they're Republican or Democrat, and vote every which way . . . most reporters, when you get to know them, fall in the general category of kind of common-sense moderates. . . . I don't think 'liberal' or 'conservative' mean very much any more. . . ." Thrum, thrum.

So much of today's reporting centers on scandal and violence that some conventional journalists are able to say, We try to wake you up; we want you to face unpleasant events that you might otherwise ignore. But those journalists start thrumming whenever a conservative attempts to connect tragic events with trendy worldviews. For example, unless we believe that ideas do not have consequences, there is a connection between Susan Smith's drowning of her children and the cheapening of young life brought about by convenient abortion. Unless we believe that life is controlled by a wheel of fortune, there is a connection between supposedly random killings by teenagers who have never known family life and the spread of feminist thinking that undermines families.

In *World*, we try to make connections. Some of our articles will wake up readers in ways that may be painful at times, but we know that the heavens declare the glory of God and the streets display the sinfulness of man; our goal is to show both. We will probably make some mistakes, but we will not go thrum, thrum.

Cabin Pressure Dropping

BY MARVIN OLASKY
JUNE 22, 1996

Since I've been traveling so much on airplanes recently, I've repeatedly heard instructions on how to use the oxygen masks that drop automatically from the ceiling in case of a decrease in cabin pressure. To get the flow of oxygen started, the attendant always says, "Give the mask a firm tug."

Firm tugs are essential. The mask will not work unless oxygen is running through the tube. So it is in American society: Accurate information is the oxygen of the body politic. In every election cycle Christians and conservatives pour millions of dollars into candidates' campaigns and then complain as liberal media undermine those candidacies. Why don't we first make sure that the flow of oxygen is clear and strong?

On Independence Day this year, as we reflect on both the American Revolution and the reasons why the political revolution of the 1980s and 1990s is now bogged down, media differences should stand out. The most influential journalists eleven score years ago were on George Washington's side; today they side with Washington's liberal bureaucracy and distribute misinformation about conservatives.

Is anyone still skeptical about charges of media bias? Look at last month's Roper survey that showed Washington bureau chiefs and congressional correspondents voting for Bill Clinton over George Bush in 1992 by a 13-to-1 ratio, and Democrats outnumbering Republicans 12 to 1 among those capital mainstays willing to state party affiliations. That's an amazing figure, given that twice as many Americans identify themselves as conservative rather than liberal.

Does anyone still believe the line from reporters of the left whenever they are confronted with such statistics—that personal attitudes do not matter, because professional reporters lay aside their own views? As the *Washington Post's* token moderate, James Glassman, notes, "That the press itself (along with the whole hand-wringing professional apparatus of our trade) chooses to gloss over it, is conclusive evidence of how pernicious the bias is." Dozens of books—I've written a few myself—show that journalists' attitudes affect not only coverage of events, but the even more crucial matter of what to cover.

What do Christians and conservatives do about the problem? Complain, mostly. Ignore it, some. Some of us gain solace by believing that a media end-around (talk radio, the Internet) and some jawboning (point out press errors) will save the day. Some cite the 1994 congressional upheaval as evidence that emphasizing elections over media can work, but that looks more and more like a fluke. And some are lullabied by publications that pretend to be neutral on their news pages.

One example of the pretense: Newspapers regularly order reporters not to march in parades for abortion and other sacraments of the left. But Malcolm Gladwell of the *Washington Post* gave the public relations rationale for this gag rule. With "a staff as totally unrepresentative of the national debate over abortion as ours is," Mr. Gladwell said, it's necessary to have "a rule about not marching in a pro-abortion protest because the whole staff could conceivably be there."

It's beginning to look as if many Christians and conservatives will keep overlooking the lack of oxygen flow—unless establishment media folks help us out by becoming so overt in their bias that it becomes impossible to ignore. One of the pleasures of living in Austin, Texas, is that our denizens of the left are more straightforward than their Washington counterparts. And last month the *American-Statesman*, Austin's monopoly daily, showed its colors by offering, without any real news hook, a massive tribute to Lyndon Johnson's endangered domestic policy legacy. For three days, more of the initial pages of the newspaper were devoted to Great Society propaganda than to all other news.

Good, I say. Other newspapers should also follow a truth-in-advertising policy, with reporters encouraged to march wherever they wish; if the whole staff heads to a rally for abortion, so be it. Maybe that would lead the rest of us to concentrate on developing more and better publications and programs. Maybe more people would realize that relying on liberal publications while concentrating on electing conservative candidates or promoting conservative ideas will not work.

Cabin pressure is decreasing yearly, but the powers of the press play on. On Independence Day 2006 or 2016, will most Americans still be dependent on secular liberal publications for the flow of oxygen we need to survive?

Journalists Need Critical Thinking

BY MARVIN OLASKY
JULY 20, 1996

Involving or exercising careful judgment." That's a definition of the word *critical* presented by the *Oxford English Dictionary*, and it's one that I and my fellow journalists should absorb. When kings and queens of the press pass along allegations without exercising critical thinking, we become pawns. But when we adopt a double standard, our credibility also is undermined.

The press was properly critical last week of unproven claims that President Clinton carried out adulterous trysts at the Washington Marriott. This and other charges of Clinton perversity emerged in a new book by former White House FBI agent Gary Aldrich; Aldrich made some talk show appearances, but NBC and CNN canceled plans to interview him.

A remembrance of vendettas past, however, should leave us skeptical concerning the extent of media righteousness. In 1991, why did Anita Hill's suddenly-revealed, unsubstantiated allegations of decade-old sexual harassment warrant sixty-seven network evening news stories even before Senate hearings examined the evidence? In 1992, why did Joe Trento's claim that a deceased ambassador had said President Bush might have slept with a State Department aide make it onto ABC and CBS without undergoing critical verification?

Reliable publications stress the work of reporters trained to evaluate sources, but some stories apparently cause editors to lose self-control. Conservative publications that present as fact mere speculation about the Clintons should be ashamed of themselves. Every little breeze may whisper Louise, as the old song goes, but journalists should investigate and watch for lawsuits instead of gossip before rushing to judgment.

Liberal publications are far more powerful in America today than conservative ones, so they have caused far more mischief. In 1991 *Time*, *Newsweek*, the *New York Times*, and many other newspapers hyped on their covers and front pages Kitty Kelley's unproven anti-Reagan allegations. Jonathan Alter, a personable *Newsweek* columnist, was defensive about his magazine's use of Ms. Kelley's work: "Of course there are some mistakes in it. . . . The point, however, is that Kelley's portrait is not essentially untrue." I haven't heard such comments from pro-Clinton journalists about Mr. Aldrich's work. A double standard trumps consistent critical thinking.

The right approach is to assign reporters to verify or knock down rumors of adultery, as the *Miami Herald* rightly did in Gary Hart's case. A similar type of critical thought should consistently be applied to public opinion poll data. Analysts know that slight changes in phrasing can radically shift poll results, but most publications still report most public opinion polls at face value—unless the polls show results sharply opposed to what journalists want to see.

For example, the respected Harte-Hanks Texas Poll last month found that 83 percent of Texans surveyed answered no to the question, "Should colleges and universities in Texas use race as a factor in admissions decisions?" Only 13 percent said yes. The poll showed 73 percent of Hispanics and 64 percent of blacks opposed to race-based decisions. Much of the *Austin American-Statesman's* report on the poll dealt with why—in the words of an inside-page headline: "Wording in race poll may have swayed its results." That's true, and similar cautions should accompany most poll results. Now, when polls come out politically correct, journalists tend to report them as revelation to which all should bow.

While on leave from The University of Texas over the past eighteen months and spending too much time back east, I was interviewed about 260 times; so I saw big chunks of the Washington press corps in action. Some of the folks are very nice, but almost all seem to paint by numbers. As CBS news correspondent Bernard Goldberg notes, "The old argument that the networks and other 'media elites' have a liberal bias is so blatantly true that it's hardly worth discovering anymore. No, we don't sit around in dark corners and plan strategies on how we're going to slant the news. We don't have to. It comes naturally to most reporters."

The liberal journalistic elite and the conservative wannabe elite both need to learn to do what does not come naturally. All of us have sinned and fall short of the glory of God. All of us need to become conscious of our own tendencies to rush to judgment. We all need to approach critically our own biases and those of our sources, and to look at the record rather than assuming either the best or the worst about political leaders—and ourselves.

World's Purpose

Schaeffer: A One-Man Wrecking Crew

BY JOEL BELZ
APRIL 14, 1986

An atrium is one of my favorite architectural distinctives. There's something about getting rid of the ceiling and lifting my eyes that prompts my heart to soar. Some people like wide, open spaces. I like wide, open entry-ways and tall hotel lobbies.

To some people, of course, an atrium is a waste. Just think of all the square feet of space that could be used or rented out if it hadn't been squandered on a high ceiling.

I am thankful—and I believe all Christians should be thankful—that the late Francis A. Schaeffer didn't think that way. Although I never talked to him about the subject, I have a hunch Francis Schaeffer probably liked atriums.

For, you see, Schaeffer spent a great deal of his life as a one-man wrecking crew, tearing out the ceiling that had existed over the room where most Christians lived when he was young. By tearing out that ceiling, Schaeffer enlarged the room in significant ways. He stretched the vision of thousands of Christians.

Schaeffer's ideas were by no means brand-new. But he stated them at a time when a student generation was ready to hear them. And, especially when you consider how complex a man Schaeffer was, he stated the ideas with remarkable simplicity and clarity.

Schaeffer explained that for the Christian there is no "upstairs" and no "downstairs." We don't deal with God in a loft at the top of a ladder and then come down to deal with the real world. For Schaeffer, it was all one room. And the God Schaeffer served and witnessed to filled that room.

That concept, of course, is central to the mission of *World* magazine. Some people wonder: Is this magazine secular or spiritual? Can't it decide which side it wants to come down on? The best answer is that we have decided—or perhaps that we've de-sided. There aren't two sides, just as there aren't two floors. "The earth is the LORD's, and the fulness thereof" (Psalm 24:1, KJV).

So what is this awkwardness our readers feel? Let us confess: We feel it too. It's one thing to say that it's all one room. But when we've been taught otherwise by centuries of tradition, habit, and practice, we don't immediately know how to treat world news as if it all belonged to the Lord.

Developing a Christian worldview is hard work, and never an all-at-once achievement.

Evangelism: You Don't Need a Lead-in Topic

BY JOEL BELZ
NOVEMBER 10, 1990

Still another *World* reader told me last week the kind of story our editorial staff likes to hear.

On a flight to the West Coast, our friend had his new copy of *World* on the empty seat beside him. A seatmate asked if she could read it, noting she'd never seen the magazine before.

One thing led to another. Before my friend knew it, the conversation had drifted through the contents of one of the articles, on to the implications of the Christian perspective in that article, and finally to the meaning of the Gospel itself. The seatmate was not a believer but was very open to the discussion.

"That was exciting," said my friend. "I was glad for the way *World* opened that door for me to witness."

We were glad too, because such a full-orbed view of how all of life hangs together is exactly what *World* seeks to promote in the hearts, minds, and behavior of readers.

It should go without saying that *World* doesn't divide life into things that are *sacred* on the one hand and things that are *secular* on the other. Because God created all things, everything in the world is sacred.

But there's a logical extension of that perspective that profoundly affects our view of evangelism. While some people understandably use all sorts of things—including *World* magazine—as lead-ins to the Gospel, a more accurate perspective is that, properly construed, you can talk about anything at all within God's wide creation and be talking evangelistically. If you are at all alert, and if your view of the world is as holistic as the Bible's is, you can talk about politics or art or science or the economy— and it all finally comes back to a discussion about God and his dealings with the people he's put here on earth. The late Francis Schaeffer masterfully modeled that kind of witness, both personally and through his extensive writing ministry.

So someone with a truly biblical perspective never limits the discussion to "evangelism." And such a person never really tries, in an ultimate sense, to move the conversation from other topics toward evangelism. He knows that he is always speaking evangelistically, because he is always speaking about the relationship of God to people. If he isn't, he should be.

But, someone will protest, don't we ultimately have to move toward closure on all these issues? Don't we have to bring people to a point of decision?

The apostle Paul, speaking on Mars Hill, provided a worthy pattern. There he seems to have been comfortable discussing all the latest ideas (current events, we might say) and the poets of Athens (please note *World*'s arts and media pages). But those subjects didn't come up just as bridges or a means of establishing rapport before turning the speech to the really important topic.

No, when Paul talked about those things, that *was* the important topic. He wasn't just hoping to sneak up on people so he could ultimately talk them into giving their hearts to Jesus. He wanted their hearts, their minds, their souls—what we have come to call a *worldview*—all to be saturated with the person of Christ.

Many of us have grown up in a generation where evangelism is geared primarily to the personal nature of Christ's offer of salvation. Yet what makes that personal offer so stupendous is precisely that it links the new believer to all the power of an infinite God who rules over every other aspect of life as well. Indeed, it is the very realization of that comprehensive power that, in the New Testament, brought person after person to what we think of as the point of decision. It wasn't an abstract or theoretical realization. People actually saw Christ's power in all its breadth and scope.

Acts 17 says "a few" believed what Paul said and followed him. Not, you might say, a noteworthy crusade statistic. But you can bet they had their worldview right. We pray in the same way for the woman on the airplane.

Doing Your Homework

BY JOEL BELZ
FEBRUARY 15, 1992

You can't remember what you never knew. That fact sooner or later will put a lot of people in jeopardy when they come face to face with God.

God tells us repeatedly in the Bible to remember his mighty acts. That involves two steps: You have to know the acts themselves, and you have to recognize them as coming from God.

We live in a time when people's ignorance on both fronts is profound. Most people are ignorant, first, of the simple facts of what is happening in the world. They are ignorant as well of the reality that what is happening is God's doing.

That means, bluntly, that most people will never be able to praise God the way he wants them to.

All this involves one of the main tasks of a magazine like *World*. In a sense, our ultimate mission is to help people praise God as they ought.

So, following the simple two-step outline noted above, *World's* assignment has two parts. First, we need to help readers know and be conversant with the details of what God is doing. That means, in good journalistic parlance, helping them know the who, the what, the when, the where, the why, and the how.

We find that repeatedly in Scripture. The Psalmist, for example, knew the details of Israel's frequent deliverances—and he knew those details so well he could rehearse them again and again hundreds of years later. Such remembering brought praise to God—but it would have been just theoretical and boring if the vivid details hadn't been part of the account. We can infer that it's important to learn the details of world affairs and to pass them on to our children and others we have responsibility to teach. Such details might properly even be seen as part of "all the counsel of God" (Acts 20:27, KJV).

A big implication is that your acquaintance with people, with events, with geography, with history, and even with ethics and philosophy are no longer just optional interests. All these subjects take on new importance because you realize you can't ultimately give God the praise he's due until you have tucked away some real acquaintance with the details of his work. Not that we're all obligated to become Ph.D.'s in esoteric subjects. But neither can we casually let ourselves off the hook by saying, "Well, I just was never very good with maps, you know." Now you see a map as the geographic outline of something God has done, one more reminder to remember.

Christians may well be as deficient as the population at large on this score. There's little evidence to suggest that believers take world affairs all that much more seriously than unbelievers do. But they should.

A second level of this perspective, however, is probably even more important. A believer's perpetual instinct should not so much be to ask, "I wonder what's happening today" as to ask, in effect, "I wonder what God's been doing today." In a profound way, the difference between those two questions boils down to a matter of whether the person involved has a heart of praise.

It's possible to cultivate such a heart. You can enhance your sense of praise, even in this terribly secular age, by daring to give God public credit for what you believe deep in your heart he has actually done. That means, when you see a magnificent sunset, you specifically thank God instead of muttering a mealy-mouthed reference to Mother Nature. It means explicitly noting God's involvement with current affairs rather than referring blandly to the way things worked out, as we are so prone to do. (President Bush's State of the Union recognition that Desert Storm was won "by the grace of God" was a refreshing, if altogether too rare, example.)

It takes surprising courage to do something so simple in company where most people have only a secular bent of mind. We're afraid of being known as crackpots or fanatics.

Yet when we fail to mention our great God in such casual conversation, we do something worse than silencing the witness we ought to be giving. We reinforce even in our own minds the inclination that God is really just a distant force, an abstraction who doesn't ultimately matter. That's a bad enough way to think now. It will be much worse when, as we stand before him face to face and he asks us to recall his mighty acts, we can't remember what we never knew.

Shooting the Rapids

BY MARVIN OLASKY
MAY 6, 1995

World has been moving in a new journalistic direction over the past three years, and we have enjoyed the favorable response, with circulation increasing threefold during that period. In response to invitations to define that new direction, our reaction generally has been, "Read our pages, not our lips." However, since we are unveiling a new design with this issue, it seems appropriate to begin explaining more explicitly the way we are attempting to challenge the conventional journalistic mind-set.

Within that mind-set, there are two kinds of stories—subjective and objective. The subjective article, commonly known as an editorial or a column, presents the opinion of one person or an editorial board. The objective account, commonly known as a news story, balances subjectivities: A statement by Advocate X is followed by an opposing statement from Advocate Y.

In practice, this objectivity has limitations: Reporters have never felt the need to balance anti-cancer views with pro-cancer responses. In recent practice, social biases have become more influential—for example, secular liberal reporters have seen pro-life concerns as cancerous—and the balancing act often farcical. Many reporters privately acknowledge that they put their hands on the scales but try to do so in subtle ways unnoticed by readers.

At *World*, we reject both the theory and the farce. Biblically, there is an alternative to both subjectivity and supposedly neutral objectivity, and it is God's perspective as given to us in the Bible. God's statements are not matters of opinion, and there is no need to balance them with another opinion. That was Eve's error. The Christian journalistic goal should be true, biblical objectivity, defined as the presentation of God's point of view.

We and all people, of course, are unable to fulfill that goal, since we are all sinners with fallen wills and very limited understanding. Nevertheless, at *World* we do not give up. The Koran calls Allah "inscrutable," but the Bible shows God revealing his thoughts to man. Much remains hidden, as Job learned, and much we see darkly, as the apostle Paul pointed out. Still, we do have some sight, and when we study the Bible to see what God says about issues, we can come closer to that God's-eye view on some issues.

Here's a metaphor we've found useful in trying to avoid the wimpiness of saying that all views require equal time and the arrogance of pretending to know God's will when the Bible is not clear: The issues that journalists report are whitewater rapids ranging in difficulty of navigation from class 1 (easy enough for a novice) to class 6 (death with a roar).

A class 1 rapids issue is one concerning which the Bible is explicit (adultery, for example); this does not mean that we plan to run anti-adultery sermons, or avoid the imperative to be accurate and fair in our narrative, description, and quotation. But we see no need to balance specific detail that shows the sad consequences of adultery with detail that makes sexual liberation seem desirable.

Clarity decreases progressively with other rapids classes. Class 2 stories are those that involve an implicit biblical position (for example, the importance of Christian education). Class 3 stories are those in which partisans of both sides can quote scriptural verses, but careful study allows biblical conclusions; welfare reform is an example.

Class 4 stories do not provide us with a clear biblical path but do allow us to bring to bear significant historical experience concerning what works and what does not. For example, we have reason to be suspicious of the person who says, "I'm from the government, and I'm here to help you." On class 5 issues there is no clear biblical mandate and no clear historical trail, but a Bible-based understanding of human nature may be helpful.

Class 6 issues are those in which there is no clear biblical position, no historical trail for the discerning to apply, and not much else to mark our path. On issues of this kind—NAFTA may have been one—*World* articles will not suggest that there is a biblical position, although we will try to use biblical understanding to sort out the relevant questions.

This six-fold framework for biblical objectivity suggests a way to push hard while avoiding Scripture-twisting. A very strong biblical stand on a class 1 or class 2 issue is objective, but a more balanced position on a class 5 or 6 issue is desirable. We approach objectivity if we faithfully reflect the biblical view—and we always fall short.

What we try to keep in mind during this process is that many rapids are class 1 or 2. One of the great contributions of the Protestant Reformation was its emphasis on the perspicuity (literally, the "see-through-ableness") of Scripture. All Christians are commanded to search the Scriptures (2 Timothy 3:15-17; Acts 17:11; John 5:39; etc.). It is bad to mistake hard rapids for easy ones, but experienced Christian journalists who read the Bible faithfully can have confidence in their ability to paddle aggressively through most rapids without being thrown into freezing water.

Accuracy and fairness are always essential; fear is not. There is no need to approach every issue as if it were a class 6.

To Soar and Surprise: Directed Reporting

BY MARVIN OLASKY
JUNE 3, 1995

The beloved Benjamin and I were playing with a Frisbee in our front yard in Austin when the mailman arrived with the new issue of *World*. After a super-hectic several months of Washington work and traveling, this was a golden moment: Benjamin at four demonstrated good eye-hand coordination by jumping for a Frisbee and actually catching it, and teenage sons Pete and David showed good brain-hand coordination by diving into *World* (my major perk as editor is that I get multiple copies).

The Frisbee, for those not familiar with one of the rare good products of the 1960s, can be thrown straight or curving, as a flutter or like a knife cutting through butter. The winds affect its flight so that no one session of Frisbee-throwing is exactly like the next, just as the news affects a news magazine so that what we anticipate at the beginning of a week is sometimes not what we are focusing on at the end.

Benjamin throws a Frisbee well except when he becomes intent on throwing it hard. That's when he holds on to it too long and ends up with an angled-right crash into the ground. A few evangelical publications do the same when they try to play "guts frisbee," a game of throwing hard at point-blank range. They have headlines such as "Christians, Stand Up to Save America from Comrade Clinton"—but they end up with an off-target embarrassment.

The more common evangelical press error, however, parallels what Benjamin did when he initially encountered a Frisbee. Just as he could not decide which hand to use in throwing, so some Christian magazines stutter: "On the one hand the Bible says x, on the other hand y." They end up, like Benjamin at first, weakly pushing out the Frisbee with both hands— and it falls to the ground, a dying dove.

Our goal at *World* is biblical objectivity. That means a goal of implicit Christocentric content in every story. Our worldview can come out in a variety of ways: by showing how man without God is a beast, by showing how Christians can build God's kingdom through putting biblical precepts into practice, by exposing ungodly leaders and programs, by showing how we can enjoy what God has given. . . . But our news reports aim to suggest God's truth by showing biblically the world he has created, not by giving a hard sell that will turn off teenagers (as well as most octogenarians), and not by dithering so that we leave readers confused.

"Show, don't tell" is a good piece of advice for all reporters, and especially for Christians. God tells us to taste and eat, to see whether his teaching is good in practice; and that is the same invitation we make to our readers. At *World* our goal is to provide the aromatic food of sensational facts and understated prose, and then allow readers to taste and eat.

We do not want to pile everything on a reader's plate, however. Our goal is *directed reporting*, which means biblical *direction* to help us see which of the thousands of facts concerning any particular story are significant, and detailed *reporting* of what we find. An article based on directed reporting is factually accurate and solidly researched, but it has a clear point of view. At *World*, as I've written previously, the goal is not to emphasize personal opinion but to provide, as best we fallen sinners can, the God's-eye perspective found in the Bible.

Directed reporting is designed to show readers the salient facts in Bible-based contextualization and to allow them to agree or disagree with the conclusions reached. The task is complicated by our desire to make reading *World* interesting and even fun, not an onerous duty. It's like playing with a Frisbee. With a four-year-old, the idea is to send the disc back and forth in a straight line, so he learns how to catch and throw; an occasional curve or flutter adds delight. Some tricky throws do go awry; the hurler shouts out "sorry," and the game goes on.

At *World*, we hope to entertain as well as crusade. Sometimes we'll make mistakes, but we'll keep going. Since we are meant to glorify God and enjoy him forever, we hope to begin doing both right now by showing God's glory and helping readers to enjoy his merciful provision.

A Monument of Infamy and Derision

BY MARVIN OLASKY
JUNE 8, 1996

Occasional readers of *World* might be mystified by some of our page headings and story headlines, and even our faithful subscribers—the most theologically literate, historically knowledgeable, and altogether terrific magazine audience on the planet—may wonder. So here is a brief lexicon that leads into a discussion of the Supreme Court's latest seizure of power.

"Publick Occurrences Both Foreign and Domestick," the heading on page 7 of each issue, is a tribute to the first American newspaper, published under that name in 1690 by Benjamin Harris. Harris, a Puritan, had come to Boston one step ahead of London police who wished to imprison him (for a second time) for criticizing royal officials. Harris was the forerunner of hard-hitting Christian journalists such as John Peter Zenger and Samuel Adams who with their pens fought corrupt leaders and also pinned down the false prophets who condoned evil in high places.

"Remarkable Providences," the heading on this page each issue, is the working definition of news that most American journalists used through

1840. Three-fourths of American newspapers and magazines from colonial days to that date were explicitly Christian, and editors saw their goal as recording what God had wrought. "Providences" were anything that happened in the world, good or bad, since all was within God's sovereignty. For example, Massachusetts ministers in 1681 urged careful coverage of "Illustrious Providences, including Divine Judgements, Tempests, Floods, Earth-quakes, Thunders as are unusual, Strange Apparitions, or what ever else shall happen that is Prodigious, Witchcrafts, Diabolical Possessions, Remarkable Judgements upon noted Sinners: eminent Deliverances, and Answers of Prayer."

The headline for this article, "A Monument of Infamy and Derision," quotes from a statement Samuel Adams made in 1776, one month after the Declaration of Independence. Adams wrote, "We have fled from the political Sodom; let us not look back, lest we perish and become a monument of infamy and derision to the world!" As our cover story suggests, the political Sodom is now all around us, and in this year of our Lord 1996 six justices of the Supreme Court are intent on making the world safe for sodomy.

Those six justices in the *Romer* case, like seven of their predecessors in *Roe v. Wade* twenty-three years ago, allowed their personal views or quests for *Washington Post* popularity to overwhelm not only the godliness that Christians hope to see in high places, but the basic discipline to which judges should aspire. Following the *Romer* decision newspaper editorialists, also like their predecessors twenty-three years ago, spent one day cheering for the Court and then declared the debate over. From now on, liberal journalists suggested, all should fall in line behind the vision of a brave new society that the Court has conjured up.

World will not fall in line. Our Christian journalistic predecessors used their limited graphic capacity to mourn the death of American liberty by Britain's Stamp Act aggression; pictured on this page is a typical "tombstone" front page from 1765. Today we have greater technological options, so *World* cartoonist Rich Bishop has been able to give us a more colorful front-page protest. But the intent is the same. We, like our predecessors, will fight with whatever journalistic tools God gives us.

"Were the talents and virtues which Heaven has bestowed on men given merely to make them more obedient drudges, to be sacrificed to the follies and ambition of a few?" That's what Samuel Adams asked 220 years ago, and most Christians answered with a "no" heard around the world. Some Christians then cried peace, peace when there was no peace, and some do now, but let us not be fooled: Infamy and derision are in the saddle, and we will either ride hard for liberty and virtue or be ridden down the path to destruction.